Contents

Chapter 1

Company Final Accounts

Questions involving company final accounts are always included on the examinations.

It is essential that you practise the questions within the allowed time frame. Lay out the Profit & Loss Account in blank form using a double page and the Balance Sheet in similar form. Enter all the figures as they appear on the question in their correct position, but place them on the left-hand page of the double page and proceed down through the Trial Balance in this manner.

Trading and Profit & Loss Accounts for the Year Ended 31 December 2001

Left-Hand Page	Right-Hand Page
1,000,000	Sales/Turnover
300,000	Less Cost of Sales
850,000	Opening Stock
	Purchases

Similarly, in the Balance Sheet, continue down until all your figures are entered.

Students may use Format 1 (discussed below) or any other appropriate format when answering Question 1, which will be for internal use. There may be other shorter questions that would specify accounts for publication, i.e. Format 1.

The only path to success with these types of questions is plenty of practice, regardless of which layout you use.

There are numerous different adjustments that will appear in these questions. The following is a summary of some of the more usual ones that will appear.

1. Goods sent on sale or return, i.e. on approval, and included in Credit Sales and in Debtors. These are, in fact, goods and should be thus recorded.
   Therefore: Sales – at Selling Price
   Debtors – at Selling Price
   Stock (twice) + at Cost Price

2. Goods bought on sale or return and included in Credit Purchases and Creditors. These are not our goods and should be excluded.
   Therefore: Purchases – at Cost Price
   Creditors – at Cost Price
   Stock – at Cost Price

3. Goods purchased and in transit but not recorded. These are the company's goods and should be included.
   Therefore: Purchases + at Cost Price
   Creditors + at Cost Price
   Stock + at Cost Price

4. Items that may be titled 'Fixed Percentage Balance Sheet Items', e.g. 10 per cent preference share capital €400,000:
   Enter under 'Capital' in Balance Sheet and Total Preference Dividend of €40,000 under 'Appropriations'. If you then discover €15,000 preference dividend paid, it follows that there is a current liability of €25,000 preference dividend unpaid.
   For 11 per cent debentures €300,000:
   Enter under 'Loans Greater Than One Year/Long-Term Liabilities' and then enter €33,000 interest in the Profit & Loss Account. If there is, for example €11,000 paid, then there is a current liability of €22,000.
   For 12 per cent investments €200,000:
   Enter as 'Financial Fixed Asset'. Then there is income in the Profit & Loss Account of €24,000. If there is an amount of €10,000 received, then there is a current asset of €14,000.

5. For errors and amounts included in other figures, use 'T' accounts as far as possible and show all your work. This will ensure that you will at least score fairly high marks, and in fact, you will have a much better chance of securing full marks.

6. Depreciation and disposals must be worked through showing each figure as in a full depreciation question.

7. Capital items entered as expense items, e.g. extension to premises constructed using own workforce and materials taken from company's stores; €50,000 Labour; €70,000 Stocks.
   Therefore: Wages €50,000
   Purchases €70,000
   Premises + €120,000.

Format 1
Companies Amendment Act 1986

Profit & Loss Account

1. Turnover
2. Cost of Sales
3. Gross Profit
4. Distribution Costs
5. Administrative Expenses
6. Other Operating Income
7. Operating Profit
8. Exceptional item – profit on sale of land
9. Interest receivable
10. Income from financial assets
11. Interest payable

Balance Sheet

A. Fixed Assets
   1. Intangible Assets
   2. Tangible Assets
   3. Financial Assets
B. Current Assets
   1. Stocks
   2. Debtors
   3. Cash/Bank
   4. Investments (short term)
C. Creditors: Amounts Falling Due within One Year
   1. Debenture Loans

Format 1 *Continued*

Profit & Loss Account	Balance Sheet
12. Profit on ordinary activities before taxation	2. Bank Loans and Overdrafts
13. Taxation on profits from ordinary activities	3. Trade Creditors, etc.
14. Profit on ordinary activities after taxation	D. Net Current Assets/Liabilities
15. Dividends paid	E. Total Assets Less Current Liabilities
16. Dividends proposed	F. Creditors: Amounts Falling Due after One Year
17. Retained profit for year	G. Provisions for Liabilities and Charges
18. Profit brought forward at 1/1/2000	H. Capital and Reserves
19. Profit carried forward at 31/12/2001	1. Called-Up Share Capital
	2. Share Premium
	3. Revaluation Reserve
	4. Other Reserves
	5. Profit & Loss

Question 1.1

Ballindine Ltd has an authorised share capital of €960,000 divided into 560,000 ordinary shares of €1 each and 400,000 11 per cent preference shares of €1 each. The following Trial Balance was extracted from its books at 31 December 2001.

Entry	Debit (€)	Credit (€)
Issued Capital: Ordinary Shares		450,000
Preference Shares		200,000
Profit & Loss		18,000
Stocks (including heating oil €1,500)	48,500	
Debtors & Creditors	55,400	63,200
Buildings at Cost	495,000	
Delivery Vans (cost €160,000)	105,000	
12% Debentures		125,000
Provision for Bad Debts		2,000
Bank		34,000
Light and Heat	5,000	
Purchases & Sales	590,000	830,000
9% Investments (1/1/2001)	150,000	
Salaries & General Expenditure	86,700	
Audit Fees	14,000	
Insurance of Vans (including suspense)	5,800	
Advertising (incorporating 4 months' investment income)	18,000	
Interim Dividends for 6 Months	28,000	
Debenture Interest Paid for First 4 months	5,500	
Directors' Fees	35,300	
Goodwill	80,000	
	1,722,200	1,722,200

You are also given the following information.

1. Stock at 31 December 2001 was valued at €52,300. This includes heating oil of €900 and stocks that cost €4,000 and have a net realisable value of €2,500.

2. The Suspense figure arises because an incorrect figure was entered for Debenture interest (although the correct figure has been entered in the bank account) and Purchases Returns €800 were entered only in the creditors account.
3. Goods sent to a customer on approval on 31 December 2001 had been entered in error as a credit sale. The selling price of these goods was €4,500, which represents cost plus 50 per cent mark-up.
4. Repairs to delivery vans costing €3,000 were carried out by the firm's own workforce. €500 of this represented parts taken from the firm's own stocks, and the remainder represented salary paid.
5. Provide for Depreciation at the rate of 20 per cent of cost per annum from date of purchase to date of sale. On 31 July 2001 a van that had cost €15,000 on 1 April 1998 was traded against a new van costing €20,000. An allowance of €6,000 was received for the old van. The cheque for the net amount was treated in error as a purchase of trading stock, and this was the only entry made in the books.
6. The directors recommend
   (a) the preference dividend due be paid,
   (b) a final dividend of 10 per cent be paid on the ordinary shares,
   (c) provision be made for debenture interest due and
   (d) a bad debt of €400 be written off and the provision for bad debts be adjusted to 4 per cent of the remaining debtors.

You are to prepare the
(a) Trading and Profit & Loss Accounts for the year ended 31 December 2001 and the
(b) Balance Sheet at 31 December 2001.

Solution to Q 1.1

Ballindine Ltd
Trading and Profit & Loss Accounts for the Year Ended 31 December 2001

	Workings	(€)	(€)	(€)
Sales			825,500	
Less Costs				
Opening Stock		47,000		
Purchases		574,700		
		621,700		
Closing Stock		52,900		
			568,800	
Gross Profit			256,700	
Investment Income	W5		13,500	
Profit on Disposal			1,000	
				271,200
Less Expenses				
Establishment & Administration				
Light & Heat	W2	5,600		
Salaries & General		84,200		
Directors' Fees		35,300		
			125,100	

Ballindine Ltd *Continued*

	Workings	(€)	(€)	(€)
Financial				
Audit Fees		14,000		
Bad Debt		400		
Increase in Provision		20		
Selling and Distribution			14,420	
Van Insurance	W3	7,100		
Delivery Van Repairs		3,000		
Depreciation for Year		32,417		
Advertising	W4	22,500	65,017	204,537
Operating Profit				66,633
less interest	W6			15,000
Net Profit				51,633
less Appropriations				
Ordinary Dividend		Paid	17,000	
		Proposed	45,000	(62,000)
Preference Dividend		Paid	11,000	
		Proposed	11,000	(22,000)
				(32,337)
Add P & L Balance 1/1/2001				18,000
P & L Balance 31/12/2001				(14,337)

Balance Sheet at 31 December 2001

	Workings	Cost (€)	Depreciation (€)	Net Book Value (€)
Fixed Assets				
Buildings		495,000		495,000
Vans	W1	165,000	77,417	87,583
		660,000	77,417	582,583
9% Investment				150,000
Goodwill				80,000
				812,583
Current Assets				
Stock			52,900	
Debtors		50,500		
Less Provision for Bad Debts		(2,020)	48,480	
Stock of Heating Oil	W2		900	
Investment Income Due	W5		9,000	
			111,280	

Balance Sheet at 31 December 2001 *Continued*

	Workings	Cost (€)	Depreciation (€)	Net Book Value (€)
Current Liabilities				
Creditors		63,200		
Bank		34,000		
Debenture Interest Due	W6	10,000		
Ordinary Dividend Due		45,000		
Preference Dividend Due		11,000		
Working Capital/Net Current Assets			163,200	(51,920)
				760,663
Financial by		Authorised	Issued	
OSC		560,000	450,000	
11% Preference Shares		400,000	200,000	
		960,000		650,000
Reserves				
Profit & Loss				(14,337)
Long-Term Liabilities				
12% Debentures				125,000
				760,663

Workings

W1

	Cost (€)	Depreciation (€)	Net Book Value (€)
Vans	160,000	(55,000)	105,000
	(15,000)	10,000	(5,000)
	20,000		
Depreciation on Old Van			
1998 $15{,}000 \times 20\% \times \frac{3}{4} =$	2,250		
1999–2000 $15{,}000 \times 20\% \times 2 =$	6,000		
2001 $15{,}000 \times 20\% \times \frac{7}{12} =$	1,750		
	10,000		
Depreciation for Year			
$145{,}000 \times 20\% =$	29,000		
$15{,}000 \times 20\% \times \frac{7}{12} =$	1,750		
$20{,}000 \times 20\% \times \frac{5}{12} =$	1,667		
	32,417		

W2

Light & Heat

(€)		(€)
1,500	Profit & Loss	5,600
5,000	Balance	900
6,500		6,500
Balance 900		

W4

Advertising

	(€)		(€)
	18,000	Profit & Loss	22,500
Investment	4,500		
	22,500		22,500

W3

Van Insurance (including suspense)

(€)		(€)
5,800	Profit & Loss	7,100
500		
800		
7,100		7,100

W5

Investment Income

	(€)		(€)
Profit & Loss	13,500	Advertising	4,500
		Balance	9,000
	13,500		13,500
Balance	9,000		

Ballindine Limited

Format 1 Solution (Published Accounts Format)
Profit & Loss Account for the year ending 31 December 2001

Turnover	825,500
Cost of Sales	(568,800)
Gross Profit	256,700
Distribution costs	(65,017)
Administrative Expenses	(139,520)
Operating Profit	52,163
Profit on disposal	1,000
Income from Financial Assets	13,500
Interest Payable	(15,000)
Profit before Taxation	51,663
Taxation	Nil
Profit after Taxation	51,663
Dividends Paid	(28,000)
Dividends Proposed	(56,000)
Retained Profit	(32,337)
Profit brought forward at 1/1/2001	18,000
Profit carried forward at 31/12/2001	(14,337)

Ballindine Limited

Format 1 Solution
Balance Sheet at 31/12/2001

Fixed Assets		
Intangible		80,000
Tangible		582,583
Financial		150,000
		812,583
Current Assets	111,280	
Creditors: Amounts falling due within one year	163,200	
Net Current Assets		(51,920)
		760,663
Financed by		
Creditors: amounts falling after one year		125,000
Share Capital		650,000
Reserves: Profit & Loss		(14,337)
		760,663

Notes to the Accounts.

1. The accounts have been prepared under the historical cost convention.
2. Stock has been valued at the lower of cost and net realisable value using the First In First Out methed of valuation.
3. Cost of Sales

Stock 1/1/2001	47,000
Purchases	574,700
Less Closing Stock	(52,900)

4. Operating Profit. The Operating Profit has been arrived at after charging

Directors' Fee	35,300
Audit Fees	14,000
Depreciation	32,417

5. Dividends

Ordinary	Paid	17,000
	Proposed	45,000
Preference	Paid	11,000
	Proposed	11,000

6. Fixed Assets

	Motor Vehicles	Buildings	Total
Cost (value 1/1/2001)	160,000	495,000	655,000
Disposal	(15,000)	–	(15,000)
Acquired	20,000	–	20,000
Value 31/12/2001	165,000	495,000	660,000

Depreciation			
Balance 1/1/2001	55,000	–	55,000
Disposal	(10,000)	–	(10,000)
Charge for year	32,417	–	32,417
Balance 31/12/2001	77,417	–	77,417
Written down value 31/12/2001	87,583	495,000	582,583

7. Intangible Fixed Assets Goodwill €80,000
8. Financial Fixed Assets 9% Investments 150,000
   Income from the investments €13,500 pa.
9. Current Assets:

Stock	52,900
Debtors	48,480
Stock of oil	900
Income due	9,000

10. Creditors: amounts falling due within one year

Trade creditors	63,200
Bank	34,000
Interest	10,000
Dividends	56,000

11. Creditors: amounts falling due greater than one year
    12% Debentures €125,000

W6

Debenture Interest

	(€)		(€)
	5,000	Profit & Loss	15,000
Balance	10,000		
	15,000		15,000
		Balance	10,000

Question 1.2

Farrell Ltd has an authorised capital of €900,000 divided into 700,000 ordinary shares of €1 each and 200,000 12 per cent preference shares of €1 each. The following Trial Balance was extracted from its books on 31 December 2000.

Issued Capital	(€)	(€)
500,000 Ordinary Shares @ €1 each		500,000
120,000 12% Preference Shares @ €1 each		120,000
Buildings at Cost	450,000	
Delivery Vans (cost €150,000)	105,000	
Purchases and Sales	720,000	900,000
Debtors and Creditors	31,400	30,200
Provision for Bad Debts		1,600
Stocks (1/1/2000)	33,600	
General Expenses (including salaries)	95,800	
Profit & Loss Balance (1/1/2000)	7,100	
Investment Income for 6 Months (incorporating formation expenses €5,000)		1,000
11% Debentures (2003/04)		84,000
10% Investments (purchased on 1/4/2000)	120,000	
Bank		16,000
Interim Dividend for First 6 Months	40,000	
Discount (Net)	1,400	
Insurance (incorporating suspense)	4,500	
Directors' Fees	15,000	
Delivery Van Expenses	12,200	
Rent	12,000	
Debenture Interest Paid for First 4 Months	2,800	
Calls in Arrears	2,000	
	1,652,800	1,652,800

The following information and instructions are to be taken into account.

(i) Stock at 31 December 2000 at cost was €39,500. This figure includes damaged stock that cost €1,800 but that is now worth €500.

(ii) The Suspense figure arises as a result of the incorrect figure for debenture interest and bad debts €400 written off against the provision for bad debts entered only in the Provision for Bad Debts Account.

(iii) Repairs to delivery vans amounting to €1,200 were carried out during the year by the firm's employees. An amount of €500 of this expenditure consisted of parts taken from the firm's trading stocks, and the remainder represented salaries.

(iv) Trading goods with a sales value of €3,500 were received from a supplier during December 2000 on a 'sale or return' basis. These goods had been incorrectly treated in the books as a credit purchase of stock at a mark up of 25 per cent on cost.

(v) Provide for depreciation on delivery vans at the annual rate of 20 per cent of cost from date of purchase to date of sale.

On 30 June 2000 a delivery van which had cost €15,000 on 1 May 1998 was traded against a new van which cost €18,000. An allowance of €7,000 was made for the old van. The cheque for the net amount of this transaction was incorrectly treated as a purchase of trading stock, and this was the only entry made in the books in respect of this transaction.

(vi) Included in the payment for insurance is an annual premium for cash-in-transit insurance of €1,200 which commenced on 1 October 2000.

(vii) The directors recommended that
- (a) provision be made for the preference dividend due,
- (b) a final dividend be provided on the ordinary shares, bringing the total dividend up to 10 per cent,
- (c) provision be made for debenture interest due,
- (d) provision be made for investment income due,
- (e) the provision for bad debts be adjusted to 5 per cent of debtors and
- (f) the formation expenses be written off over a five-year period commencing in 2000.

You are required to prepare the

(a) Trading, Profit & Loss and Appropriation Accounts for the year ended 31 December 2000 and the

(b) Balance Sheet at 31 December 2000 (modern format).

Solution to Q 1.2

Farrell Ltd
Trading, Profit & Loss and Appropriation Accounts for the Year Ended 31 December 2000

	(€)	(€)	(€)
Sales			900,000
Less Cost of Sales			
Stock (1/1/2000)		33,600	
Purchases		705,700	
		739,300	
Less Stock (31/12/2000)		35,400	703,900
Gross Profit			196,100
Add Investment Income			9,000
Reduction in Provision for Bad Debts			50
			205,150
Less Expenses			
Establishment & Administration			
General Expenses (including salaries)	95,100		
Insurance	3,420		
Rent	12,000		
Directors' Fees	15,000	125,520	
Financial			
Debenture Interest	9,240		
Discount (net)	1,400		
Cash-in-Transit Insurance	300	10,940	
Selling & Distribution			
Delivery Van Expenses	13,400		
Loss on Sale of Van	1,500		
Depreciation on Delivery Vans	30,300	45,200	181,660
Net Profit			23,490
Less Balance (1/1/2000)			(7,100)
			16,390
Less Appropriations			
Formation Expenses		1,000	
Preference Dividend — Interim	7,200		
— Due	7,200	14,400	
Ordinary Dividend — Interim	32,800		
— Final	17,200	50,000	65,400
Balance (31/12/2000)			(49,010)

Farrell Ltd
Balance Sheet at 31 December 2000

	Cost (€)	Depreciation (€)	Net (€)
Fixed Assets			
Buildings	450,000		450,000
Delivery Vans	153,000	68,800	84,200
	603,000	68,800	534,200
10% Investments			120,000
Current Assets			
Stock		35,400	
Debtors	31,000 – 1,550	29,450	
Investment Income Due		3,000	
Insurance Prepaid		900	
		68,750	
Less Current Liabilities			
Creditors	27,400		
Bank	16,000		
Debenture Interest Due	6,160		
Preference Dividend Due	7,200		
Ordinary Dividend Final	17,200	73,960	(5,210)
			648,990
Financed by			
Authorised Share Capital			
700,000 Ordinary Shares @ €1 each			
200,000 12% Preference Shares @ €1 each			
Issued Share Capital			
500,000 Ordinary Shares @ €1 each			500,000
Less Calls in Arrears			(2,000)
			498,000
120,000 12% Preference Shares @ €1 each			120,000
			618,000
Reserves			
Profit & Loss Balance		(49,010)	
Less Formation Expenses		(4,000)	(53,010)
Shareholders' Funds			564,990
Long-Term Liabilities			
11% Debentures			84,000
			648,990

Question 1.3
The Trial Balance of Traytown Plc at 31 December 2000 is as follows.

	Dr (€'000)	Cr (€'000)
Share Capital		20,000
Profit & Loss Account		6,250
Revaluation Reserve		1,500
Freehold Buildings — Valuation	12,000	
Plant and Equipment — Cost	5,500	
Motor Vehicle — Cost	2,300	
Provision for Depreciation — Freehold Buildings		960
Provision for Depreciation — Plant and Equipment		1,100
Provision for Depreciation — Motor Vehicles		460
Stocks (1/1/2000)	9,500	
Sales		108,000
Purchases	82,000	
Wages and Salaries	6,500	
Directors' Remuneration	320	
Social Welfare Costs	720	
Other Pension Costs	330	
Auditors' Remuneration	85	
Interest Payable on Overdraft	650	
Administrative Expenses	4,200	
Distribution Costs	6,400	
Bank Deposit Interest Received		120
Rent Received		340
Trade Debtors	15,000	
Sundry Prepayments	240	
Cash at Bank	720	
Trade Creditors		4,100
Bank Overdraft		2,700
PAYE		220
PRSI		175
Sundry Creditors		540
	146,465	146,465

The following information is also provided.

1. Authorised share capital is 20,000,000 ordinary €1 shares, allotted and fully paid.
2. Stocks at 31 December 2000 are valued at €7,200,000.
3. Provide for depreciation on cost or valuation of fixed assets, all of which were purchased

before 1 January 2000 as follows:

	% per annum
Freehold Buildings	2
Plant and Equipment	10
Motor Vehicles	20

4. Wages and Salaries, Social Welfare Costs, Other Pension Costs and Depreciation are to be apportioned equally between Administration and Distribution.
5. An action is pending against the company in respect of a claim for faulty goods amounting to €1,500,000. The company's directors and legal advisors are of the view that the claim is unlikely to succeed.
6. Freehold Buildings were valued at 31 December 2000 by P. Jones & Co Chartered Surveyors, Dublin. The open market valuation is €15,000,000.
7. A dividend of 10 cent per share is proposed.
8. Corporation tax for the year, payable on 31 July 2001, is €1,400,000.

Prepare the

(a) Profit & Loss Account for the year ended 31 December 2000 and the
(b) Balance Sheet at 31 December 2000, in accordance with Formal 1, Companies Act.

Solution to Q 1.3(a)

Traytown Plc
Profit & Loss Account for the Year Ended 31 December 2000

	(€'000)
Turnover	108,000
Cost of Sales	84,300
Gross Profit	23,700
Distribution Costs	(10,800)
Administration Expenses	(9,005)
Other Operating Income	340
Operating Profit	4,235
Interest Receivable	120
Interest Payable	(650)
Profit before Taxation	3,705
Taxation	(1,400)
Profit after Taxation	2,305
Dividends	2,000
Retained Profit	305
Balance 1/1/	6,250
Balance 31/12/	6,555

Solution to Q 1.3(b)

Traytown Plc
Balance Sheet at 31 December 2000

	(€'000)	(€'000)	(€'000)
Fixed Assets			
Tangible Assets		20,230	
Current Assets			
Stocks	7,200		
Debtors	15,240		
Cash at Bank and in Hand	720		
		23,160	
Creditors: Amounts Falling Due within One Year		11,135	
Net Current Assets		12,025	
		32,255	
Capital and Reserves			
Called-Up Share Capital		20,000	
Profit & Loss Account		6,555	
Revaluation Reserve		5,700	
		32,255	

Question 1.4

Grogan Ltd has an authorised capital of €900,000 divided into 600,000 ordinary shares at €1 each and 300,000 10 per cent preference shares at €1 each. The following Trial Balance was extracted from its books on 31 December 2001.

	(€)	(€)
Profit & Loss Balance (1/1/2001)	8,600	
Issued Capital		
400,000 Ordinary Shares at €1 each		400,000
200,000 10% Preference Shares at €1 each		200,000
Buildings at Cost	451,000	
Delivery Vans (cost €140,000)	95,000	
Stocks	37,600	
Debtors and Creditors	50,200	43,300
9% Investments (1/1/2001)	160,000	
8% Debentures		90,000
Bank		22,000
Purchases and Sales	660,000	880,000
Provision for Bad Debts		1,600
Salaries and General Expenses	99,800	
Discount (net)		5,400

Continued

Continued

	(€)	(€)
Directors' Fees	24,000	
Rent	9,800	
Debenture Interest Paid for First 4 Months	2,500	
Advertising (incorporating suspense)	7,400	
Goodwill (incorporating 3 months' investment income)	12,400	
Interim Dividends for First 6 Months	24,000	
	1,642,300	1,642,300

The following information and instructions are to be taken into account.

1. Stock at 31 December 2001 at cost was €42,600. This figure includes damaged stock that cost €3,300 but that now has a net realisable value of €1,300.
2. Goodwill, which incorporates a quarter year's investment income, is to be written off over a five-year period commencing in 2001.
3. The Suspense figure arises as a result of the incorrect figure for debenture interest (although the correct entry has been made in the bank account) and discount received of €350 entered only in the Creditors Account.
4. Provide for depreciation on delivery vans at the annual rate of $12\frac{1}{2}$ per cent of cost from the date of purchase to the date of sale. No entry was made in the books for the following; on 31 December 2001, a delivery van which cost €12,000 on 30 June 1995, was traded against a new van which cost €28,000. An allowance of €5,000 was made on the old van. The cheque for the net amount of this transaction was incorrectly treated as a purchase of trading stock. This was the only entry made in the books in respect of this transaction.
5. During 2001 a store, which cost €20,000, and stock, which cost €6,000, were destroyed by fire. A new store was built by the firm's own workers. The cost of their labour, €9,500, was treated as a business expense and the materials, costing €25,500, were taken from the firm's stocks. The insurance company has agreed to contribute €26,000 to compensate for the fire damage. No adjustments were made in the books in respect of the old or new store.
6. The directors recommended that
   (a) the preference dividend due be paid,
   (b) a final dividend on ordinary shares be provided bringing the total dividend up to 15 per cent,
   (c) provision be made for income and interest due and
   (d) provision for bad debts be adjusted to 4 per cent of debtors.

You are required to prepare the

(a) Trading, Profit & Loss and Appropriation Account for the year ended 31 December 2001 and the
(b) Balance Sheet at 31 December 2001.

Solution to Q 1.4

Grogan Ltd
Trading, Profit & Loss and Appropriation Accounts for the Year Ended 31 December 2001

	(€)	(€)	(€)
Sales			880,000
Less Cost of Sales			
Stock (1/1/2001)		37,600	
Add Purchases		605,500	
		643,100	
Less Stock (31/12/2001)		40,600	602,500
Gross Profit			277,500
Add			
Investment Income			14,400
Discount			5,750
Profit on Sale of Van			2,750
			300,400
Less Expenses			
Administration Expenses			
Salaries and General Expenses	90,300		
Directors' Fees	24,000		
Rent	9,800		
Goodwill written off	3,200	127,300	
Selling and Distribution Expenses			
Provision for Bad Debts	408		
Depreciation Delivery Vans	19,000		
Advertising	7,850	27,258	153,058
Operating Profit			147,342
Less Debenture Interest			7,200
			140,142
Less Appropriations			
Interim Preference Dividend		10,000	
Interim Ordinary Dividend		14,000	
Proposed Preference Dividend		10,000	
Proposed Ordinary Dividend		46,000	(80,000)
			60,142
Less Profit & Loss Balance (1/1/2001)			(8,600)
Balance			51,542

Balance Sheet at 31 December 2001

	Cost (€)	Depreciation to Date (€)	Net (€)
Fixed Assets			
Buildings	466,000		466,000
Delivery Vans	156,000	52,750	103,250
	622,000	52,750	569,250
Investments			
9% Investments			160,000
Intangible Assets			
Goodwill			12,800
			742,050
Current Assets			
Stock		40,600	
Debtors		48,192	
Investment Income Due		10,800	
Insurance Company		26,000	
		125,592	
Less Current Liabilities			
Creditors	43,300		
Preference Dividend Due	10,000		
Ordinary Dividend Due	46,000		
Debenture Interest Due	4,800		
Bank	22,000	126,100	(508)
			741,542
Financed by	Authorised	Issued	
Ordinary Shares at €1 each	600,000	400,000	
11% Preference Shares at €1 each	300,000	200,000	
			600,000
Reserves			
Profit & Loss Balance		51,542	
		651,542	
Long-Term Liabilities			
8% Debentures		90,000	
		741,542	

Question 1.5

The Trial Balance of Paycomp Plc at 31 December 2000 is as follows.

	Dr (€'000)	Cr (€'000)
Share Capital		10,000
Revaluation Reserve		5,000
Profit & Loss Account		3,040
Freehold Buildings — Valuation	15,000	
Plant and Machinery — Cost	3,000	
Motor Vehicles — Cost	1,200	
Provision for Depreciation — Freehold Buildings		1,500
— Plant and Machinery		900
— Motor Vehicles		480
Stocks (1/1/2000)	8,400	
Sales		73,000
Purchases	45,000	
Wages and Salaries	7,000	
Social Welfare Costs	860	
Other Pension Costs	210	
Directors' Salaries	670	
Auditors' Remuneration	75	
Motor — Travelling Expenses	3,200	
Expenditure on Research	120	
General Administrative Expenses	2,400	
General Distribution Expenses	1,900	
Interest Paid	1,300	
Rents Received		640
Interest Receivable (bank deposits)		320
Trade Debtors	15,420	
Prepayments	170	
Cash at Bank	310	
Trade Creditors		2,400
Bank Loan		8,500
PAYE		125
PRSI		110
Accruals		220
	106,235	106,235

You are also provided with the following information.

1. Authorised share capital is 10,000,000 ordinary shares of €1 each, allotted and fully paid.
2. Stocks at 31 December 2000 are valued at €7,200,000.
3. Freehold Buildings were valued at 31 December 2000 by K. Smith & Co, Chartered Surveyors, Dublin. The open market valuation is €20,000,000.
4. Interest paid is on the Bank Overdraft and Bank Loan, which is repayable within five years.
5. Provide for depreciation on cost or valuation of fixed assets, all of which were purchased

before 1 January 2000 as follows:

	% per annum
Freehold Buildings	2
Plant and Machinery	10
Motor Vehicles	20

6. Wages and Salaries, Motor and Travelling Expenses and Depreciation should be apportioned equally between Administration and Distribution.
7. Expenditure on Research represented the cost in the year of applied research on the development of a new product. Management is confident that this product will be successful.
8. A dividend of 20 cent per share is proposed.
9. Corporation tax for the year, payable on 31 July 2000, is €3,500,000.

Prepare the

(a) Profit & Loss Account for the year ended 31 December 2000 and the
(b) Balance Sheet at 31 December 2000 both in the published accounts format.

Solution to Q 1.5

Paycomp Plc
Profit & Loss Account for the Year Ended 31 December 2000

	(€)	(€'000)
Turnover		73,000
Cost of Sales		(46,320)
Gross Profit		26,680
Distribution Costs		(7,955)
Administrative Expenses		(9,200)
		9,525
Other Operating Income		640
Operating Profit		10,165
Interest Receivable		320
Interest Payable		(1,300)
Profit on Ordinary Activities before Taxation		9,185
Tax on Profit on Ordinary Activities		(3,500)
Profit for the Financial Year		5,685
Dividends Paid and Proposed		(2,000)
Profit Retained in Year		3,685
Balance at Beginning of Year		3,040
Balance at End of Year		6,725

Paycomp Plc
Balance Sheet at 31 December 2000

	(€'000)	(€'000)
Fixed Assets		
Tangible Assets		22,280
Current Assets		
Stocks	7,200	
Debtors	15,590	
Cash at Bank and in Hand	310	
	23,100	
Creditors (amounts falling due within one year)	(8,355)	
Net Current Assets		14,745
Total Assets Less Current Liabilities		37,025
Creditors (amounts falling due after one year)		8,500
		28,525
Capital and Reserve		
Called-Up Share Capital		10,000
Revaluation Reserve		11,800
Profit & Loss Account		6,725
		28,525

+ Notes (show any of 6)

Question 1.6

The Trial Balance of Garfen Plc at 30 June 2001 is as follows.

	Dr (€'000)	Cr (€'000)
Share Capital		2,000
Profit & Loss Account		900
Freehold Buildings — Cost	1,400	
Plant and Equipment — Cost	350	
Motor Vehicles — Cost	700	
Provisions for Depreciation — Freehold Buildings		210
— Plant and Equipment		105
— Motor Vehicles		140
Stocks (1/7/2000)	1,560	
Debtors	857	
Unlisted Investments	360	
Cash at Bank	220	
Trade Creditors		725
Bank Overdraft		670
Income from Investments		25
Bank Deposit Interest Received		19
Sales		14,500

(Continued)

Continued

	Dr (€'000)	Cr (€'000)
Purchases	8,800	
Wages and Salaries	1,100	
Interest Paid on Overdraft	140	
Directors' Salaries	600	
Auditors' Remuneration	57	
Administrative Expenses	950	
Distribution Costs	2,200	
	19,294	19,294

The following information is also provided.

1. Authorised share capital is 2,000,000 ordinary €1 shares, allotted and fully paid.
2. Provide for depreciation on cost of fixed assets, all of which were purchased before 1 July 2000 as follows:

	% per annum
Freehold Buildings	2.5
Plant and Equipment	10
Motor Vehicles	20

3. Stocks at 30 June 2001 are valued at €1,650,000
4. Wages and Salaries and Depreciation are to be apportioned equally between Administration and Distribution Expenses.
5. A dividend of €0.10 per share is proposed.
6. On 7 July 1993 a notice of liquidation of a debtor owing €75,000 was received. Garfen Plc is unlikely to receive anything in respect of this debt.
7. Corporation tax for the year, payable on 31 December 2001, is €180,000.

Prepare the

(a) Profit & Loss Account for the year ended 30 June 2001 and the
(b) Balance Sheet at 30 June 2001 in accordance with Companies Act Format 1.

Solution to Q 1.6(a)

Garfen Plc
Profit & Loss Account for the Year Ended 30 June 2001

	Workings/Notes	(€)	(€)
Turnover			14,500
Cost of sales			8,710
Gross Profit			5,790
Distribution Costs			(2,855)
Administrative Expenses			(2,337)
Operating Profit			598
Income from Financial Assets	W1		25
Other Interest Receivable	W2		19
Interest Payable	W3		(140)
Profit on Ordinary Activities before Taxation	W4		502
Tax on Profit on Ordinary Activities			(180)
Profit for the Financial Year			322
Dividends Proposed	W5		(200)
Profit Retained in Year			122
Balance at Beginning of Year			900
Balance at End of Year			1,022

Solution to Q 1.6(b)

Garfen Plc
Balance Sheet at 30 June 2001

	Workings/Notes	(€)	(€)
Fixed Assets			
Tangible Assets	W6		1,785
Financial Assets	W7		360
			2,145
Current Assets			
Stocks			1,650
Debtors	W8	782	
Cash at Bank			220
			2,652
Creditors (amounts falling due within one year)	W9	1,775	
Net Current Assets			877
			3,022

Continued

Continued

	Workings Notes	(€)	(€)
Capital and Reserves			
Called-Up Share Capital	W10		2,000
Profit & Loss Account			1,022
			3,022

Workings/Notes

W1. Income from Financial Assets
Income from Unlisted Investments €25

W2. Other Interest Receivable
Bank Deposit Interest €19

W3. Interest Payable
On Bank Overdraft €140

W4. Operating Profit
This has been arrived at after charging

Depreciation	€210
Directors' salaries	€600
Auditors' Remuneration	€57

W5. Dividends Proposed
Final Dividend of €0.10 per Share €200

W6. Tangible Assets

	Freehold Buildings (€)	Plant and Equipment (€)	Motor Vehicles (€)	Total (€)
Cost 1 July 2000/30 June 2001	1,400	350	700	2,450
Depreciation				
1 July 2000	210	105	140	455
Charged in Year	35	35	140	210
30 June 2001	245	140	280	665
Net Book Value 30 June 2001	1,155	210	420	1,785

W7. Financial Assets
Unlisted Investments €360

W8. Debtors
Amounts Falling Due within One Year €782

W9. Creditors

Amounts Falling Due within One Year

Trade Creditors	€725
Bank Overdraft	€670
Corporation Tax	€180
Dividends Proposed	€200
	€1,775

W10. Called-Up Share Capital

Authorised 2,000,000 Ordinary Shares of €1 Each	€2,000
Allotted and fully paid 2,000,000 ordinary shares of €1 each	€2,000

Question 1.7

The Trial Balance of Minco Plc at 31 December 2001 is as follows.

	Dr (€)	Cr (€)
Share Capital		5,000
Profit & Loss Account		4,600
Freehold Buildings — Cost	6,400	
Equipment — Cost	2,200	
Motor Vehicles — Cost	3,600	
Provisions for Depreciation — Freehold Buildings		720
— Equipment		330
— Motor Vehicles		720
Unlisted Investments	1,700	
Stocks (1/1/2001)	5,700	
Sales		28,300
Purchases	12,900	
Wages and Salaries	3,200	
Directors' Remuneration	760	
Administrative Expenses	1,200	
Distribution Costs	3,500	
Auditors' Remuneration	26	
Bank Deposit Interest Receivable		135
Income from Investments		59
Interest Payable on Overdraft	438	
Rent Receivable		360
Trade and Sundry Creditors		3,800
Debtors	4,900	
Cash at Bank	3,300	
Bank Overdraft		5,800
	49,824	49,824

The following information is also provided.

1. Authorised share capital is 5,000,000 ordinary €1 shares, allotted and fully paid.
2. Stocks at 31 December 2001 are valued at €4,200,000.

3. Provide for depreciation on cost of fixed assets, all of which were purchased before 1 January 2001, as follows:

	% per annum
Freehold Buildings	2
Equipment	10
Motor Vehicles	20

4. Wages and Salaries and Depreciation are to be apportioned equally between Administration and Distribution.
5. During the preparation of the accounts, it was discovered that the stocks at 31 December 2000 had been overstated by €550,000.
6. A dividend of €0.10 per share is proposed.
7. Corporation tax for the year, payable on 30 June 2002, is €1,900,000.

Prepare, insofar as the available information permits, the

(a) Profit & Loss Account for the year ended 31 December 2001 and the
(b) Balance Sheet at 31 December 2001, both for publication, using Format 1.

Solution to Q 1.7(a)

Minco Plc
Profit & Loss Account for the Year Ended 31 December 2001

	Workings	(€)
Turnover — Continuing Operations	W13	28,300
Cost of Sales		(13,850)
Gross Profit		14,450
Distribution Costs		(5,634)
Administrative Expenses		(4,120)
		4,696
Other Operating Income	W1	360
Operating Profit		5,056
Income from Financial Assets	W2	59
Other Interest Receivable	W3	135
Interest Payable	W4	(438)
Profit on Ordinary Activities before Taxation	W5	4,812
Tax on Profit on Ordinary Activities		(1,900)
Profit for the Financial Year		2,912
Dividend Proposed	W6	(500)
Profit Retained in Year		2,412
Balance at Beginning of Year	W7	4,050
Balance at End of Year		6,462

Solution to Q 1.7(b)

Minco Plc
Balance Sheet at 31 December 2001

	Workings	(€)	(€)
Fixed Assets			
Tangible Assets	W8		9,362
Financial Assets	W9		1,700
			11,062
Current Assets			
Stocks			4,200
Debtors	W10		4,900
Cash at Bank			3,300
			12,400
Creditors (amounts falling due within one year)	W11		(12,000)
Net Current Assets			400
			11,462
Capital and Reserves			
Called-Up Share Capital	W12		5,000
Profit & Loss Account			6,462
			11,462

Workings

W1. Other Operating Income
Rent Receivable €360

W2. Income from Financial Assets
Income from Unlisted Investments €59

W3. Other Interest Receivable
Bank Deposit Interest €135

W4. Interest Payable
On Bank Overdraft €438

W5. Profit on Ordinary Activities before Taxation
This has been arrived at after charging

Depreciation	€1,068
Directors' Remuneration	€760
Auditors' Remuneration	€26

W6. Dividends Proposed
Final Dividend of €0.10 per Share €500

W7. Balance at Beginning of Year

As Previously Reported	€4,600
Deduct Prior Year Adjustment	€550
	€4,050

The prior year adjustment arose as a result of the overstatement of the closing stock in the accounts for the year ended 31 December 2000.

W8. Tangible Assets

	Freehold Buildings (€)	Plant and Equipment (€)	Motor Vehicles (€)	Total (€)
Cost 1 January 2001/31 December 2001	6,400	2,200	3,600	12,200
Depreciation				
1 January 2001	720	330	720	1,770
Charged in Year	128	220	720	1,068
31 December 2001	848	550	1,440	2,838
Net Book Value 31 December 2001	5,552	1,650	2,160	9,362

W9. Financial Assets

Unlisted Investments €1,700

W10. Debtors

Amounts Payable within One Year €4,900

W11. Creditors

Amounts Falling Due within One Year

Trade and Sundry Creditors	€3,800
Bank Overdraft	€5,800
Corporation Tax	€1,900
Dividends Proposed	€500
	€12,000

W12. Called-Up Share Capital

Authorised 5,000,000 Ordinary Shares of €1 Each €5,000,000

Allotted and Fully Paid 5,000,000 Ordinary Shares of €1 each €5,000,000

W13.

	(€)
Cost of Sales	
Stock 1 January 2001	5,150
Purchases	12,900
	18,050
Stocks 31 December 2001	4,200
	13,850
Distribution Costs	
Per Trial Balance	3,500
Wages and Salaries	1,600
Depreciation	534
	5,634
Administrative Expenses	
Per Trial Balance	1,200
Wages and Salaries	1,600
Directors' Remuneration	760
Auditors' Remuneration	26
Depreciation	534
	4,120

Chapter 2

Ratios and Analysis

Ratios

It is essential that all the ratios are known. Even more important is the ability to comment on the significance of the ratios.

1. Gross Profit Percentage/Margin
2. Mark-Up Percentage
3. Rate of Stock Turnover
4. Net Profit Percentage/Margin
5. Length of Credit Given to Debtors
6. Length of Credit Received from Creditors
7. Interest Cover
8. Working Capital Ratio
9. Liquid Asset Ratio
10. Capital Gearing Ratio
11. Return on Capital Employed
12. Return to Equity Shareholders
13. Earnings per Share
14. Price Earnings Ratio
15. Dividend per Share
16. Dividend Cover
17. Dividend Yield

Practice writing out the ratios until you are absolutely sure that you know them all.

Indicators of Bankruptcy

The indicators of bankruptcy have been developed in the US and are called 'Z scores'. The higher the score, the less likelihood of insolvency. The results show that almost every company that failed in a particular year showed warning signs in the previous year's results.

Five ratios are used:

1. $\dfrac{\text{Working Capital}}{\text{Total Assets}}$

2. $\dfrac{\text{Retained Earnings}}{\text{Total Assets}}$

3. $\dfrac{\text{Profit before Interest and Tax}}{\text{Total Assets}}$

4. $\dfrac{\text{Market Value}}{\text{Total Debt}}$

5. $\dfrac{\text{Sales}}{\text{Total Assets}}$

When you are asked for a particular ratio, do not just write down the answer. Write down the formula in words. Then write down the first line of the formula in figures. Finally, show all your calculations to the last line. For example,

Issued Ordinary Share @ €1 €500,000
10% Preference Shares @ €1 €300,000
Net Profit €150,000
(ignore tax)

You are asked for the earnings per share.

$$\text{Earnings per share} = \frac{\text{Net Profit} - \text{Preference Dividend} - \text{Tax}}{\text{Number of Ordinary Shares}}$$

$$= \frac{150{,}000 - 30{,}000}{500{,}000}$$

$$= \frac{120{,}000}{500{,}000} = 24 \text{ cent}$$

(Note: The cent designation is essential.)

When asked to comment on the performance of the company, i.e. whether the company is a good investment either on the part of a prospective shareholder or a lending institution, it is vital that you are able to comment properly and make proper comparisons.

The following are the key areas.

1 Profitability

Profitability – Return on Capital Employed and Return to Equity Shareholder and compare to present return on risk-free investment. Compare with previous year if possible.

2 Liquidity

Current Ratio 1.5 to 2 : 1
Quick Ratio 1 : 1

3 Gearing

A lowly geared company cannot get into financial difficulty. High gearing **may** be acceptable if the company is highly profitable.

4 Trends

If you are given figures for only one year, it is very difficult to do other than look at the reserve figures. If you are given results for more than one year, there are a lot of comparisons that can be made, and it is a matter of emphasising the most important.

5 Company Sector

Comment and compare to industry norm if given.

6 Company Name

Look at company title to see if it is a Plc or a private company.

7 Fixed Assets

Look for full breakdown, giving composition and depreciation policy.

8 Debentures

Rate of interest and amount of interest and interest cover. Refer back to gearing, look at redemption date and effect on future liquidity.

9 Dividends

Dividend Cover and Yield are important to ensure that dividends are not paid out of reserves. Look at the market price of the shares. If the company is not a Plc, note that there is not a ready market for the shares.

10 Purchase of Shares

If being asked to buy shares in the company, see if the number of shares being bought would give control of the company. Look at the cost of borrowing and the present dividend policy.

11 Loan

If being asked to lend to the company, state that you must know for what purpose the finance is required and how the future Interest Cover, Capital Gearing Ratio and Liquid Asset Ratio will be affected.

12 Investments

If the company has investments compare cost and market value to see if selling these might help alleviate any liquidity problem the company might have.

13 Earnings

Look at Earnings per Share and Price Earnings Ratio, and consider the industry norm if one is given.

14 Audit

State that in order to comment fully on a particular company, you would require a full set of unqualified audited accounts for a number of years.

If the company has liquidity/profitability and you are asked to suggest some type of corrective action, you might suggest some of the following: Sale & Leaseback, Factoring of Debtors, Sale of Investment, Issue of Shares (if possible), Capital Reduction Scheme or even Closedown.

Question 2.1

The following figures have been taken from the final account of Down 'n' Out Ltd at 31 December 2001. This is a business involved in the manufacture of furniture. The authorised share capital is €960,000 made up of 500,000 €1 ordinary shares and 230,000 €2, 9 per cent preference shares.

	(€)
Sales	780,000
Cost of Sales	600,000
Total Expenses	150,000
Profit & Loss (1/1/2001)	90,000
Profit & Loss (31/12/2001)	30,000
Proposed Dividends	48,000
Fixed Assets	700,000
Current Assets (including stock €90,000)	140,000
Trade Creditors	60,000
General Reserve (1/1/2001)	40,000
10% Debentures 2002 Secured	120,000
Issued ordinary shares 300,000 @ €1 each	
Issued preference shares 100,000 @ €2 each	

(a) Calculate the following:
   (1) opening stock if the rate of stock turnover is ten times.
   (2) Price Earnings Ratio if the market price of one ordinary share is 80 cent.
   (3) Interest Cover.
   (4) Dividend Yield on one ordinary share.
   (5) Gearing Ratio and its effect on the distribution of profits.

(b) Down 'n' Out Ltd has applied to your bank for a loan of €180,000. You are the assistant lending officer. Write a report to your manager outlining your reasons for giving/not giving the loan.

Solution to Q2.1 (a)

Down 'n' Out Ltd
Trading and Profit & Loss Accounts

	(€'000)	(€'000)
Sales		780
Less Cost		600
Gross Profit		180
Less Expenses		150
Net Profit		30
+ Balance		90
		120
– Proposed Dividends		
Preference	18	
Ordinary	30	48
		72
Balance (31/2/2001)		30
To General Reserves		42
General reserve (1/1/2001)		40
General (31/12/2001)		82

Balance Sheet at 31 December 2001

	(€'000)	(€'000)	(€'000)
Fixed Assets			700
Current Assets			
Stock	90		
Drs, etc.	50	140	
Current Liabilities			
Creditors	60		
Dividends	48	108	
NCA			32
			732
Financed by			
Ordinary Shares		300	
9% Preference		200	
		500	
Reserves			
General Reserve	82		
Profit & Loss	30	112	
10% Debentures		120	
			732

(1) Rate of Stock Turnover $= \dfrac{\text{Cost of Sales}}{\text{Average Stock}} = 10$

$$= \frac{600}{x} = 10$$

Therefore

$$x = 60$$

and if

$$\text{closing stock} = 90$$

then

$$\text{opening stock} = 30$$

(note a 300 per cent increase)

(2) Price Earnings Ratio = $\dfrac{\text{Market Price}}{\text{Earnings per Share}}$

$$\text{Earnings per Share} = \frac{\text{Net Profit} - \text{Preference Dividend}}{\text{Number of Ordinary Shares}}$$

$$= \frac{30 - 18}{300} = 4 \text{ cent}$$

$$\text{Price Earnings Ratio} = \frac{80}{4} = 20 \text{ times}$$

(3) Interest Cover = $\dfrac{\text{Net Profit} + \text{Interest}}{\text{Interest}}$

$$= \frac{30 + 12}{12} = 3.5 \text{ times}$$

(4) Dividend Yield = $\dfrac{\text{Dividend per Share}}{\text{Market Price}} \times \dfrac{100}{1}$

$$\text{Dividend per Share} = \frac{\text{Ordinary Dividends}}{\text{Number of Ordinary Shares}} = \frac{30}{300} = 10 \text{ cent}$$

$$\text{Dividend Yield} = \frac{10}{80} \times \frac{100}{1} = 12.5\%$$

(5) Gearing Ratio and Debt/Equity Ratio

Preferences Shares + Debentures : Ordinary Shares
200 + 120 : 300
320 : 300
1.07 : 1

The company is highly geared, and this burden must be met before there is anything available for the equity holders.

Solution to Q2.1 (b)

To:
From:
Date:
Re: Loan to Down 'n' Out of €180,000

Down 'n' Out are well named, and I would not advance the loan for the following reasons.

(i) The Return on Capital Employed is only 5.74 per cent. Even in times of low interest rates, this is not acceptable and is less than the return achievable on risk-free investments.

(ii) The company has liquidity problem. The current ratio is 1.3 : 1, which is well below the norm of 2 : 1. The Liquid Asset Ratio is only 0.46 : 1, which is well below the desired figure of 1 : 1.

(iii) The company is in the furniture-manufacturing business, which is extremely competitive and cyclical. The stock during the year has increased by 300 per cent, indicating a high build up of slow moving stock.

(iv) Dividends are being maintained but are being paid out of reserves, while the company is trying to borrow money to solve its liquidity problems.

(v) The debentures are due for repayment within the next twelve months and there are no liquid assets for this purpose; this is probably, in part, why the loan is being requested.

(vi) The Interest Cover at present is only 3.5 times. Further borrowing will only reduce this at least in the short term.

(vii) The actual value of any fixed assets offered as security must be doubtful, and the debenture holders at present have a prior security.

(viii) The firm's Z scores (predictors of bankruptcy) are generally poor

$$\frac{\text{Working Capital}}{\text{Total Assets}} = \frac{32}{840}$$

$$\frac{\text{Retained Earnings}}{\text{Total Assets}} = \frac{112}{840}$$

$$\frac{\text{Operating Profit}}{\text{Total Assets}} = \frac{42}{840}$$

$$\frac{\text{Market Value}}{\text{Total Debt}} = \frac{240}{320}$$

$$\frac{\text{Sales}}{\text{Total Assets}} = \frac{780}{840}$$

Note: The actual value of the fixed assets and the stock must be questioned.

(ix) The company is not a Plc, and this makes it less attractive as a lending proposition.

(x) The company is already highly geared, and further borrowing will in the short term at least only increase this high gearing and place an even bigger burden on the firm.

(xi) To even consider lending to this company in future, a clear explanation of why the finance is required would have to be given, together with three to five years of unqualified audited accounts. Even then, it is doubtful if this company would be a good lending proposition.

Question 2.2

The following are the summarised final accounts of two manufacturing companies, Soda Ltd and Tonic Ltd, for the year ended 31 December 2001.

Summarised Profit & Loss Accounts for the Year Ended 31 December 2001

	Soda Ltd		Tonic Ltd	
	(€)	(€)	(€)	(€)
Sales		700		540
Cost of Goods Sold		310		230
Gross Profit		390		310
Debenture Interest	40		20	
Other Expenses	190	230	140	160
Net Profit		160		150

Balance Sheet at 31 December 2001

	(€)	(€)	(€)	(€)
Fixed Assets at Cost		820		370
Accumulated Depreciation		360		80
		460		290
Current Assets				
Trade Debtors	115		60	
Stocks	80		40	
Bank	10			
	205		100	
Current Liabilities				
Trade Creditors	80		55	
Net Current Assets		125		45
		585		335
Financed by				
Shareholders' Funds		345		220
Debentures		240		115
		585		335

The following information is also available.

1. Approximately 90 per cent of each company's sales are made on credit.
2. Each company's stock level remains approximately constant throughout the year.

Requirement: Write a report to the managing director of Soda Ltd comparing the performance of her company with that of Tonic Ltd. Your report should include reference to appropriate ratios and any other information that you consider relevant.

Solution to Q 2.2
Your answer should be put into report format with comments on the following.

	Soda Ltd	Tonic Ltd
Gross Profit (%)	55.71	57.41
Net Profit (%)	22.86	27.78
Return on Capital Employed	34.19	50.75
Expenses/Sales (%)	32.86	29.63
Interest Cover	5	8.5
Working Capital Ratio	2.56 : 1	1.82:1
Liquid Asset Ratio	1.56:1	1.09 : 1
Credit to Debtors (days)	66	45
Credit from Creditors (days)	94	87
Stock Turnover	3.88	5.75
Working Capital/Total Assets	0.19	0.12
Debt/Equity	0.7 : 1	0.52 : 1

Question 2.3
The following figures have been taken from the final accounts of Gill plc, a wholesaler in home computers and games software, whose authorised capital is €1,000,000 made up of 800,000 ordinary shares at €1 each and 100,000 8 per cent preference shares at €2 each. The firm has already issued 500,000 ordinary shares and 50,000 preference shares.

	(€)
Fixed Assets (cost €500,000)	490,000
Investments (market value €80,000)	160,000
Current Assets (Stock €200,000, Debtors €69,000)	269,000
Current Liabilities (Bank €2,000, Trade Creditors €90,000)	92,000
General Reserve (1/1/2002)	25,000
9% Debentures 2004 secured	90,000
Sales	920,000
Opening Stock	58,000
Cost of Sales	730,000
Total Expenses for the Year	96,000
Profit & Loss Balance (1/1/2002)	18,000 CR
Profit & Loss Balance (31/12/2002)	12,000 CR
Proposed Dividends	32,000

(a) Calculate the following:
  (i) Dividend per Ordinary Share.
  (ii) Interest Cover.
  (iii) Market Value of One Ordinary Share whose Dividend Yield is 5 per cent.
  (iv) Cash Sales if the average period of credit is 1.2 months.
  (v) Price Earnings Ratio.

(b) Would the shareholders be satisfied with the policies, performance and state of affairs of the above company? Use relevant ratios and information to support your answer.

(c) Comment on the liquidity of Gill plc and suggest appropriate action.

Solution to Q 2.3(a)

(i) Dividend per Ordinary Share

$$\frac{\text{Ordinary Dividend}}{\text{Number of Ordinary Shares}} = \frac{24{,}000}{500{,}000} = 4.8 \text{ cent}$$

(ii) Interest Cover

$$\frac{\text{Net Profit + Interest}}{\text{Interest}} = \frac{94{,}000 + 8{,}100}{8{,}100} = 12.6 \text{ times}$$

(iii) Market Value of One Ordinary Share

$$\frac{\text{Dividend per Share} \times 100}{\text{Market Price}} = \frac{4.8 \times 100}{5 \times \text{Market Price}} = 96 \text{ cent}$$

(iv) Cash Sales

$$\frac{69{,}000 \times 12}{\text{Credit Sales}} = 1.2$$

Credit Sales = 690,000

Total Sales = 920,000

Cash Sales = 920,000 – 690,000 = €230,000

(v) Price Earnings Ratio

$$\frac{\text{Market Price}}{\text{Earnings per Share}} = \frac{96}{18.8} = 5.1 : 1$$

Solution to Q 2.3 (b)

Trends: Gill plc has increased its reserves from €43,000 at the beginning of the year to €105,000 at the end of the year. This has more than doubled its reserves even after providing for dividends amounting to €32,000. This would seem to suggest an improved performance over recent years.

Profitability: The firm's profitability is satisfactory. The Return on Capital Employed and the Return to Equity Shareholders of 12.8 and 15.9 per cent, respectively, are better than the return available at present from risk-free investments. The Earnings per Share is 18.8 cent, and it would take 5.6 years for a share to recoup its market price.

Dividend Policies: The dividends are covered 2.9 times. Therefore the shareholders are receiving 34 per cent of available profits. The policy of paying out dividends is creating cash flow problems for the company. The dividend per share is 4.8 cent and the dividend yield is 5 per cent whereas the preference shareholders receive 8 per cent.

Investment Policy: The investments have dropped 50 per cent in value from €160,000 to €80,000. This places a question mark over its investment policy.

Debentures: The debentures are due for repayment in 1996. This will put a great strain on the firm's liquidity. As the debentures are secured on the fixed assets, the repayments could place the future of Gill plc in jeopardy as the 2 per cent depreciation indicates that these assets are buildings or they are totally under depreciated and therefore the depreciation policy must be questioned.

Sector: Gill plc is involved in the home computer and games software business. This is a very competitive sector.

Closing Stock: The shareholders would be very concerned that the firm's huge closing stock is more than four times its opening stock.

Interest Cover: The Interest Cover is 12.6 times. This is a very favourable situation and indicates that borrowings are being put to good use.

Gearing: The firm is low geared as the fixed interest capital is 24 per cent of total capital employed.

The shareholders would not be satisfied with the policies and state of affairs but would be satisfied with the performance of Gill plc.

Solution to Q 2.3 (c)

The Working Capital Ratio and Acid Test Ratio are 2.2 to 1 and 0.6 to 1, respectively. The Working Capital Ratio is above the accepted norm of 2 : 1. This shows that working capital is sufficient to meet the day to day costs of running the firm. The firm should not let this go too high above 2 : 1 as this would indicate a build-up of stock or a poor use of resources.

The Acid Test Ratio is below the accepted norm of 1 : 1. This shows more accurately the ability of the firm to pay its short term debts. Gill plc would have difficulty paying its immediate debts:

1. Sell investments. Any surplus cash not required for working capital should be re-invested more profitably. Income from this would improve profitability.
2. Sell stock at an auction and raise at least €55,000.
3. Make a Right Issue of about 60,000 shares.
4. Sell some of the fixed assets and lease back.
5. Delay the payments of dividends.

Question 2.4
The Balance Sheets of J. Giles are as follows.

	31 March 2001		31 March 2002	
	(€)	(€)	(€)	(€)
Fixed Assets		260,000		205,000
Current Assets				
Stocks	86,000		84,000	
Debtors	94,000		58,000	
	180,000		142,000	
Current Liabilities	(174,000)	6,000	(59,000)	83,000
		266,000		288,000
Capital				
Opening Balance		262,900		266,000
Add Net Profit		15,600		36,000
Less Drawings		(12,500)		(14,000)
Closing Balance		266,000		288,000

The following information was extracted from the trading accounts for the years ended 31 March 2001 and 2002, respectively.

	2001 (€)	2002 (€)
Sales	505,000	385,000
Gross Profit	152,900	172,750
Opening Stock	82,000	86,000

Required: Calculate the following ratios for each year and comment on the position shown for the second year as compared with the first.

1. Gross Profit Ratio.
2. Stock Turnover.
3. Working Capital Ratio.
4. Acid Test Ratio.
5. Period of Credit Given.

Solution to Q 2.4

1. Gross Profit Ratio

= (Gross Profit × 100)/Sales

Year Ended 31 March 2001: €152,900 × 100/€505,000 = 30.3%

Year Ended 31 March 2002: €172,750 × 100/€385,000 = 44.9%

The ratios have increased form 30.3 to 44.9 per cent. Possible explanations are

(i) changes in the types of goods sold, where some lines carry different rates of gross profit than others,
(ii) increase in the selling price of goods without a proportionate increase in the cost price,
(iii) elimination of inefficiencies and factors such as theft which would reduce the profit margin.

2. Stock Turnover
= Cost of Sales/Average Stock
where Cost of Sales = Sales – Gross Profit.
Year Ended 31 March 2001: €352,100/€84,000 = 4.2 times
Year Ended 31 March 2002: €212,250/€85,000 = 2.5 times

In the first year the average stock was turned over 4.2 times. This has deteriorated to 2.5 times in the second year. This has happened because although sales and purchases have fallen considerably, stock levels have remained relatively constant. It may well be possible to reduce stock levels if this reduction is likely to be permanent.

3. Working Capital Ratio
= Current Assets : Current Liabilities
As at 31 March 2001: €180,000 : €174,000 = 1.04 : 1
As at 31 March 2002: €142,000 : €59,000 = 2.41 : 1

Current Assets were roughly equal to Current Liabilities at 31 March 2001. However, Mr Giles might have difficulty paying his liabilities on time, depending on how quickly his current assets could be turned into cash. His position at 31 March 2002 appears comfortable, with Current Assets equal to 2.41 times Current Liabilities.

4. Acid Test Ratio
= Current Assets – Stock : Current Liabilities
As at 31 March 2001: €94,000 : €174,000 = 0.54 : 1
As at 31 March 2002: €58,000 : €59,000 = 0.98 : 1

At 31 March 2001, quick assets (those readily convertible into cash) amounted to only 54 per cent of Current Liabilities. If the Current Liabilities are required to be paid promptly, Mr Giles would not be able to meet these in full. At 31 March 2002, quick assets approximately equalled Current Liabilities, and he should then have been in a position to meet the total liabilities.

5. Period of Credit Given
= (Debtors × 365)/Sales
Year Ended 31 March 2001: (€94,000 × 365)/€505,000 = 68 days
Year Ended 31 March 2002: (€58,000 × 365)/€385,000 = 55 days

The average period of credit given to customers has decreased from 68 days to 55 days. This ratio reflects the time taken by customers to pay and should approximate the credit terms allowed by the business. The situation has improved, and viewed in conjunction with the fall in sales, this would suggest that Mr Giles has been more selective in deciding to whom he sells goods on credit.

Question 2.5

You are asked to examine the financial planning policy of Straffan Ltd, a new company that is being established in the competitive agricultural processing and distribution sector. Its effective corporation tax rate will be 20 per cent. Its initial financing will be

	(€)
800,000 Ordinary Shares of €1 each	800,000
10% Debentures	400,000
Assets employed	1,200,000

The directors have adopted the following five minimum financial planning objectives:

(i) Return on Assets Employed 20 per cent per annum, i.e. Profits before Interest & Tax to Assets Employed at the beginning of each year,
(ii) Interest Cover of 6 times,
(iii) Dividend Cover of 4 times,
(iv) Earnings per Share Growth 5 per cent per annum,
(v) Debt/Equity Ratio of 1 : 2.

Required: Set out the projected earnings and assets, employing computations for the first three years and utilising the primary criteria (i)–(iii).

Solution to Q 2.5

Straffan Ltd

	Year 1 (€)	Year 2 (€)	Year 3 (€)
Ordinary Shares	800,000	800,000	800,000
Retained Earnings		120,000	254,400
Shareholders' Funds	800,000	920,000	1,054,400
10% Debentures	400,000	400,000	400,000
Capital Employed	1,200,000	1,320,000	1,454,400
Profit before Interest & Tax	240,000	264,000	290,880
(20% Return on Capital Employed)			
Debenture Interest	40,000	40,000	40,000
	200,000	224,000	250,880
Tax (20%)	40,000	44,800	50,176
	160,000	179,200	200,704
Dividend (1 : 4 cover)	40,000	44,800	50,176
Retained Earnings	120,000	134,400	150,528
Earnings Per Share Projected (cent)	20	22.4	25.1
Projected Earnings Per Share Growth (%)		11.2	12.1
Debt/Equity Projected	1 : 2.0	1 : 2.3	1 : 2.6
Interest Cover	1 : 6.0	1 : 6.6	1 : 7.27
Dividend Growth (%)		12	12

Question 2.6

Southern Stores
Trading and Profit & Loss Accounts for the Year Ended 30 June 2001

	30 June 2001 (€)	30 June 2000 (€)
Sales	420,000	250,000
Cost of Sales		
Opening Stock	75,000	
Purchases	260,000	225,000
Less Closing Stock	85,000	75,000
	250,000	150,000
Gross Profit	170,000	100,000
Overheads		
Wages	63,000	40,000
Repairs	4,000	1,500
Leasing	4,000	3,200
Telephone	4,200	3,500
Rent and Rates	15,000	10,500
Motor Expenses	3,800	4,000
Advertising	3,000	3,200
Depreciation	20,000	20,000
Insurance	6,000	5,800
Loan Interest	5,000	4,000
	128,000	95,700
Net Profit	42,000	43,000

Southern Stores
Balance Sheet at 30 June 2001

	30 June 2001 (€)		30 June 2000 (€)	
Fixed Assets		60,000		80,000
Current Assets				
Stocks	85,000		75,000	
Debtors	65,000		30,000	
Cash and Bank	1,000		0	
	151,000		105,000	

Continued

Southern Stores *Continued*

		30 June 2001 (€)		30 June 2000 (€)
Current Liabilities				
Creditors and Accruals	72,000		75,000	
Bank Overdraft	26,000		25,700	
	98,000		100,700	
Net Current Assets		5,300		4,300
		113,000		84,300
Represented by				
Capital Account				
Opening Balance	34,300			
Cash Introduced			40,000	
Plus Profits	42,000		4,300	
	76,300		44,300	
	10,300		10,000	
Capital		66,000		34,300
Long-Term Loans		4,000		50,000
		113,000		84,300

The above accounts are for Southern Stores, a business owned and run by Joe North. You are asked to work out the following ratios in relation to the accounts presented. (Please show your workings.) Each correct answer will be awarded two marks. Each incorrect answer will have one-third of a mark deducted.

1. What is the percentage increase in sales from year ended 30 June 2000 to 30 June 2001?
   (A) 54% (B) 68% (C) 74%
2. What is the Mark-Up Percentage for the year ended 30 June 2001?
   (A) 68% (B) 50% (C) 35%
3. What is the Gross Margin Percentage for the year ended 30 June 2001?
   (A) 47% (B) 30% (C) 40%
4. What is the Net Profit Percentage for the year ended 30 June 2001?
   (A) 20% (B) 15% (C) 10%
5. What was the rate of return of Net Profit on Capital Employed for the year ended 30 June 2001?
   (A) 64.2% (B) 37.17% (C) 90.1%
6. What is the Current Ratio at the year ended 30 June 2001?
   (A) 2.8 (B) 1.54 (C) 4.1
7. What is the Acid Test Ratio at the year ended 30 June 2001?
   (A) 0.67 (B) 1.04 (C) 0.88
8. What is the Stock Turnover in the year ended 30 June 2001?
   (A) 6.1 times per annum (B) 4.62 times per annum (C) 3.13 times per annum

9. What is the Debtors' Turnover in the year ended 30 June 2001?
   (A) 8.84 times per annum (B) 10.54 times per annum (C) 6.87 times per annum
10. What is the Creditors' Turnover in the year ended 30 June 2001?
   (A) 6.84 times per annum (B) 2.66 times per annum (C) 3.54 times per annum

Solution to Q 2.6

1(B) $\dfrac{\text{Increase in Sales}}{\text{Sales to 30 June 2000}} = \dfrac{170{,}000}{250{,}000} \times \dfrac{100}{1} = 68\%$

2(A) $\dfrac{\text{Gross Profit}}{\text{Cost of Sales}} = \dfrac{170{,}000}{250{,}000} \times \dfrac{100}{1} = 68\%$

3(C) $\dfrac{\text{Gross Profit}}{\text{Sales}} = \dfrac{170{,}000}{420{,}000} \times \dfrac{100}{1} = 40\%$

4(C) $\dfrac{\text{Net Profit}}{\text{Sales}} = \dfrac{42{,}000}{420{,}000} \times \dfrac{100}{1} = 10\%$

5(B) $\dfrac{\text{Net Profit}}{\text{Capital Employed}} = \dfrac{42{,}000}{113{,}000} \times \dfrac{100}{1} = 37.17\%$

6(B) $\dfrac{\text{Current Assets}}{\text{Current Liabilities}} = \dfrac{151{,}000}{98{,}000} = 1.54 : 1$

7(A) $\dfrac{\text{Current Assets} - \text{Stock}}{\text{Current Liabilities}} = \dfrac{151{,}000 - 85{,}000}{98{,}000} = 0.67 : 1$

8(C) $\dfrac{\text{Cost of Goods Sold}}{\text{Average Stock}} = \dfrac{250{,}000}{80{,}000} = 3.13$ times per annum

9(A) $\dfrac{\text{Annual Credit Sales}}{\text{Average Debtors}} = \dfrac{420{,}000}{(65{,}000 + 30{,}000)/2} = 8.84$ times per annum

10(C) $\dfrac{\text{Annual Purchases}}{\text{Average Creditors}} \; \dfrac{260{,}000}{(72{,}000 + 75{,}000)/2} = 3.54$ times per annum

Question 2.7

John Blank owns a confectionery shop. Turnover is comprised of cash sales. In January 2001, the manager of the shop suddenly disappeared. John, alarmed by this and by a serious disimprovement in the business bank balance, asked you to conduct an investigation.

You obtained the following information.

1. For the first six months of 2000, goods were sold to yield a rate of gross profit of $33\frac{1}{3}$ per cent. The rate of VAT during this period was 15 per cent.
2. From 1 July 2000 the rate of gross profit was reduced to 25 per cent and the rate of VAT was reduced to 10 per cent.

3. The quantity of goods sold in the second six months of 2000 was 50 per cent higher than in the first six months of the year.
4. Purchases for the year (excluding VAT) amounted to €520,000.
5. Stocks, valued at cost, were as follows.

	(€)
1 January 2000	60,000
31 December 2000	80,000

6. Cash lodgements in respect of sales amounted to €635,000.

You are required to calculate the amount of any cash deficiency.

Solution to Q 2.7

John Blank

Sales Second Half is 50% above First
First $\frac{2}{5}$ Second $\frac{3}{5}$

∴ Purchases in Square Ratio

First (€)	Second (€)	Total (€)	
208,000	312,000	520,000	
31,200	31,200	62,400	VAT
239,200	343,200	582,400	inc. VAT

Sales. All For Cash + VAT
Opening Stock + Purchases – Closing Stock

Cost of Sales 520,000 + 60,000 – 80,000 = 500,000
Based on *Q* of Goods not value

	First (€)	Second (€)	Total (€)	
Cost	200,000	300,000	500,000	
Mark Up	66,667	100,000	166,667	
Sales ex VAT	266,667	400,000		
+ VAT	40,000	40,000		
	306,667	+ 440,000	= 746,667	Cash
			635,000	Lodged
			€111,667	Deficiency

Chapter 3

Incomplete Records

When dealing with what are known as Type A questions, i.e. Cash/Bank Payment-type questions, it is a good idea to treat them as an exercise in basic bookkeeping.

First, enter the opening balances in general journal format to find the missing goodwill figure. Next enter all the figures in T accounts as opening balances. Then open a cash account and credit all the payments. Complete the double entry by debiting these accounts.

Do the same with the bank account, i.e. Credit all the payments and then debit the other. The main problem areas in these questions arise with loans and interest calculations and with drawings. If the amount of the loan is funded, i.e. of an endowment-type, then the total of the loan in the balance sheet will always be the original amount borrowed. If the loan is being repaid, then the amount of repayments made reduce the loan balance. Loan repayments do not go into the profit and loss account.

When allocating the figure for drawings for interest, light and heat, insurance, etc., you will be clearly instructed as to which way to calculate it — amount paid, amount used, amount payable or whatever. By using the T account format and reading the instructions carefully you will get the correct answer.

In Type B questions, you have the same difficulties as in Type A regarding loans and drawings, but you go through the question in a different manner. First, enter the opening figures in the general journal in order to find goodwill. Then enter the appropriate opening figures in the year end balance sheet/statement of affairs. Find the closing figures for stock, debtors, creditors, etc., and enter them in the balance sheet. Keep the number of accounts to a minimum, opening accounts only for expenses and drawings. Do not open a bank account. Finally, the missing balance sheet figure will be the net profit which you will use in the profit and loss account to work back to the sales figure.

In type C questions, you must know all the ratios and be able to work through them quickly. Start by opening a blank trading and profit and loss account with headings for Sales, Purchases, Closing Stock, Cost of Sales, Gross Profit, Total Expenses and Net Profit. Lay it out to take up the full page. Then, lay out a balance sheet in similar fashion. Finally, insert the figures you are given in the correct positions, and then use your knowledge of the ratios to calculate the missing figures.

There are other formats in which these questions can arise, and some are included with worked solutions.

Question 3.1 (*Type A*)
On 1 January 2001 Eddie Dunphy purchased the business of Charlton & Co for €125,000 consisting of the following tangible assets and liabilities: Premises €99,000; Stock €22,000;

Creditors €16,800; Debtors €14,900; Electricity due €540; and three months' insurance prepaid €1,500.

During 2001 Dunphy did not keep a full set of accounts but was able to supply you with the following information.

Cash Payments:	Purchases €43,400; General Expenses €28,300; Lodgements €53,000; Light & Heat €4,600.
Bank Payments:	Annual Insurance Premium €6,300; Creditors €35,000; Delivery Van €18,000; Interest €1,800; Household Furniture €5,600.
Bank Lodgements:	Lotto Win €25,000; Cash €53,000; Debtors €27,500.

During the year Dunphy took from stock goods to the value of €250 per month and cash of €600 per month.

On 1 September 2001 Dunphy borrowed €80,000, part of which was used to purchase an adjoining premises for €72,000. The rate of interest was 9 per cent per annum, payable monthly on the last day of each month. The capital sum was to be repaid in one lump sum in the year 2015, and to provide for this the bank was to pay €360 per month on the last day of each month into an investment account.

Dunphy estimated that one-third of Light and Heat used, Insurance paid and Interest payable should be attributed to the private section of the premises.

Included in the assets and liabilities of the business on 31 December 2001 were: Creditors €16,400; Stock €23,000; Debtors €15,400; Cash €680, Electricity due €500, Stock of Heating Oil €360; €25 interest earned by the fund to date.

Prepare Trading and Profit & Loss Accounts for the year ended 31 December 2001 and a Balance Sheet at 31 December 2001.

Solution to Q 3.1

E. Dunphy
Opening Entries
Method — Showing All Accounts

	DR (€)	CR (€)
Capital		125,000
Premises	99,000	
Stock	22,000	
Creditors		16,800
Debtors	14,900	
Electricity		540
Insurance	1,500	
Goodwill	4,940	
	142,340	142,340

Capital Account (1)

	(€)		(€)
		Opening Balance	125,000
		Bank	25,000

Premises Account (2)

	(€)		(€)
Opening Balance	99,000		
Loan	72,000		

Opening Stock (3)

	(€)		(€)
Opening Balance	22,000		

Total Creditors (4)

	(€)		(€)
Bank	35,000	Opening Balance	16,800
Balance	16,400	Credit Purchases	34,600
	51,400		51,400

Total Debtors (5)

	(€)		(€)
Opening Balance	14,900	Bank	27,500
Credit Sales	28,000	Balance	15,400
	42,900		42,900

Light & Heat Account (6)

	(€)		(€)
Cash	4,600	Opening Balance	540
Balance	500	Drawings	1,400
		Profit & Loss	2,800
		Balance	360
	5,100		5,100

Insurance Account (7)

	(€)		(€)
Opening Balance	1,500	Drawings	2,100
Bank	6,300	Profit & Loss	4,650
		Balance	1,050

Goodwill Account (8)

	(€)		(€)
Opening Balance	4,940		

Cash Account (9)

	(€)		(€)
Cash Sales	137,180	Purchases	43,400
		General Expenses	28,300
		Bank	53,000
		Light & Heat	4,600
		Drawings	7,200
		Balance	680
	137,180		137,180

Purchases Account (10)

	(€)		(€)
Cash	43,400	Drawings	3,000
Credit	34,600	Trading Account	75,000
	78,000		78,000

General Expenses (11)

	(€)		(€)
Cash	28,300		

Bank Account (12)

	(€)		(€)
Capital	25,000	Insurance	6,300
Cash	53,000	Creditors	35,000
Debtors	27,500	Delivery Vans	18,000
Loan	8,000	Interest	1,800
		Drawings	5,600
		Investment Fund	1,440
		Balance C/D	45,360
	113,500		113,500

Delivery Vans (13)

	(€)		(€)
Bank	18,000		

Interest (14)

	(€)		(€)
Bank	1,800	Drawings	800
Balance C/D	600	Profit & Loss	1,600
	2,400		2,400

Drawings (15)

	(€)		(€)
Bank	5,600		
Purchases	3,000		
Cash	7,200		
Light & Heat	1,400		
Interest	800		
Insurance	2,100		
	20,100		

Loan Account (16)

	(€)		(€)
		Premises	72,000
		Bank	8,000

Investment Fund Account (17)

	(€)		(€)
Bank	1,440		
Income	25		

Sales Account (18)

	(€)		(€)
Trading Account	165,180	Credit	28,000
		Cash	137,180
	165,180		165,180

Investment Income (19)

	(€)		(€)
		Fund	25

Eddie Dunphy
Trading and Profit & Loss Account for the Year Ended 31 December 2001

	(€)	(€)
Sales		165,180
Less Cost of Sales		
Opening Stock	22,000	
Purchases	75,000	
	97,000	
Less Closing Stock	23,000	
Cost of Sales		74,000
Gross Profit		91,180

Continued

Eddie Dunphy *Continued*

	(€)	(€)
Less Expenses		
Insurance	4,650	
General Expenses	28,300	
Light & Heat	2,800	
Interest	1,600	37,350
		53,830
Investment Income		25
Net Profit		53,855

Balance Sheet at 31 December 2001

	(€)	(€)	(€)
Fixed Assets			
Premises	171,000		
Delivery Vans	18,000		
Goodwill	4,940		
Investment Fund	1,465	195,405	
Current Assets			
Stock	23,000		
Debtors	15,400		
Bank	45,360		
Stock of Heating Oil	360		
Insurance Prepaid	1,050		
Cash	680		
		85,850	
Less Current Liabilities			
Creditors	16,400		
Interest	600		
Electricity Bill	500		
		17,500	68,350
Net Current Assets			263,755
Financed by			
Capital		150,000	
Plus Net Profit		53,855	
		203,855	
Less Drawings		20,100	
		183,755	
Loan		80,000	263,755

Question 3.2 (*Type B*)

On 1 January 2001 D. Swindler purchased a business for €110,000 consisting of the following tangible assets and liabilities: Premises €86,000; Stock €13,000; Debtors €11,000; Equipment €14,000; Creditors €14,000; Wages Due €2,500; Insurance Prepaid €600.

During 2001 Swindler did not keep a full set of books but was able to supply you with the following information on 31 December 2001.

1. On 1 June 2001 Swindler borrowed €60,000 from International Finance Plc, some of which was used to purchase an adjoining premises for €56,000. It was agreed that Swindler would pay interest on the last day of each month at the rate of 11 per cent per annum. The capital sum was to be repaid in one lump sum on 30 May 2016, and to provide for this, the bank was to transfer €350 on the last day of each month into an investment account, commencing immediately.
2. Each week Swindler withdrew the following for personal use: Stock €70 and Cash €90.
3. During the year the following payments were made: Insurance €2,400; Wages €18,900; Interest €3,300; Motor Vehicles €18,000; Light & Heat €4,450; Sundry Expenses €22,000. A €10,000 legacy was lodged to the business bank account.
4. Swindler estimated that one-third of the Light & Heat used, Interest payable and Insurance paid should be attributed to the private section of the premises. Two-thirds of the value of the Motor Vehicles were for private use.
5. Included in the assets and liabilities of the firm on 31 December 2001 were: Stock €15,000; Debtors €12,500; Creditors €14,500; Bank €17,000; Electricity due €470; €40 interest earned by the fund to date.
6. Swindler's Gross Profit was 30 per cent of Sales.

Prepare in as much detail as possible:

(a) Statement/Balance Sheet showing Swindler's Profit/Loss for the year,
(b) Trading and Profit & Loss Accounts for the year and
(c) Advise Swindler.

Note: Do not omit section (c) even when revising this topic. This is omitted by many students in examination.

Solution to Q 3.2

General Journal

	DR (€)	CR (€)
Capital		110,000
Stock	13,000	
Premises	86,000	
Debtors	11,000	
Equipment	14,000	
Creditors		14,000
Wages Due		2,500
Insurance Prepaid	600	
Goodwill	1,900	
	126,500	126,500

Drawings

Purchases	3,640		
Cash	4,680		
Interest	1,283		
Motor Vehicles	12,000		
Insurance	800		
Light & Heat	1,640		
	24,043		

Wages Account

Bank	18,900	Balance	2,500
		Profit & Loss	16,400

Insurance Account*

Balance	600	Drawings	800
Bank	2,400	Profit & Loss	2,200
	3,000		3,000

* Should there be a balance on account at year end?

Interest Account

Bank	3,300	Drawings	1,283
Balance	550	Profit & Loss	2,567
	3,850		3,850

Light & Heat

Bank	4,450	Drawings	1,640
Balance	470	Profit & Loss	3,280
	4,920		4,920

Loan 60,000 × 11% × 7/12 = 3,850

Balance Sheet at 31 December 2001

	(€)	(€)	(€)
Fixed Assets			
Premises (86,000 + 56,000)			142,000
Equipment			14,000
Motor Vehicles			6,000
Investment Fund (7 × 350) + 40			2,490
Goodwill			1,900
			166,390
Current Assets			
Stock		15,000	
Debtors		12,500	
Bank		17,000	
		44,500	
Less Current Liabilities			
Creditors	14,500		
ESB Bill	470		
Interest	550		
	15,520	28,980	
Net Current Assets			195,370
Financed by			
Capital (110,000 + 10,000)		120,000	
Plus Net Profit		39,413	
Less Drawings		(24,043)	
Term Loan		60,000	195,370

Trading and Profit & Loss Accounts for the Year Ended 31 December 2001

	(€)	(€)
Sales		286,067
Less Cost of Sales		
Opening Stock	13,000	
Purchases (205,887 – 3,640)	202,247	
	215,247	
Less Closing Stock	15,000	
Cost of Sales		200,247
Gross Profit		85,820
Less Expenses		
Wages	16,400	
Insurance	2,200	
Insurance	2,567	
Light & Heat	3,280	
Sundry Expenses	22,000	46,447
		39,373
Plus Fund Income		40
Net Profit		39,413

A few brief points of advise to Swindler:

(i) Employ an accountant.
(ii) Keep a full set of accounts.
(iii) Provide for depreciation.
(iv) Control Drawings.

Question 3.3 (*Type C*)
U. Chancer invested €95,000 in a new business on 1 January 2001. The following information was supplied by Chancer on 31 December 2001.

Rate of Stock Turnover (based on Closing Stock)	6 times
Drawings for the Year	€10,000
Current Ratio	2 : 1
Quick Ratio	0.5 : 1
Depreciation of Fixed Assets	€15,000
Total Expenses	€40,000
Gross Margin	25%
Average Period of Credit Given to Debtors	0.3 months
Creditors	€18,000
Cash Sales	€192,000

Current Assets consist of Stock, Debtors and Bank.
Current Liabilities comprise Creditors and Bills payable €2,000.

Depreciation is calculated at 15 per cent for a full year.
Drawings include drawings of stock €2,000.

You are required in as much detail as possible to provide

(a) Balance Sheet at 31 December 2001 and
(b) Trading and Profit & Loss Accounts for the year ended 31 December 2001.

Solution to Q 3.3(a)

Balance Sheet at 31 December 2001

	€	Cost (€)	Depreciation (€)	Net Value (€)
Fixed Assets		100,000	15,000	85,000
Current Assets				
Stock	30,000			
Debtors	6,000			
Cash	4,000	40,000		
Less Current Liabilities				
Creditors	18,000			
Bills Payable	2,000	20,000		
Net Current Assets			20,000	
			105,000	
Financed by				
Capital		95,000		
Plus Net Profit		20,000		
Less Drawings		(10,000)	105,000	

Solution for Q 3.3(b)

Trading and Profit & Loss Accounts for the Year Ended 31 December 2001

	(€)	(€)
Sales		240,000
Less Cost		
Purchases (212,000 – 2,000)	210,000	
Less Closing Stock	30,000	
Cost of Sales		180,000
Gross Profit		60,000
Total Expenses		
Depreciation	15,000	
Sundry Expenses	25,000	40,000
Net Profit		20,000

Question 3.4

Your employer's finance department has recently developed a computer model to assist in the prediction of the profit and loss account and balance sheet for the first year of trading. When the sales forecast and the values of the various parameters are entered, the model will print a summary profit and loss account and an outline balance sheet. The model parameters are as follows.

Gross Profit as a Percentage of Sales	40%
Selling Expenses as a Percentage of Sales	14%
Administration Costs (excluding interest)	€12,000
Interest Rate on Long-Term Debt	10%
Return on Capital Employed (profit before interest divided by closing capital employed)	20%
Ratio of Long-Term Debt to Equity	1 : 1
Ratio of Fixed to Net Current Assets	3 : 1
Current Ratio	2 : 1

The first trial of the model has a sales value of €100,000. The only expense items to be considered are selling, administration and interest.

You are required to prepare a forecast of the

(a) Profit Statement based on the above information using an initial sales value of €100,000 and the

(b) Balance Sheet in as much detail as possible.

Solution to Q 3.4

Profit Statement

	(€)	(€)
Sales		100,000
Less Cost		60,000
Gross Profit		40,000
Selling Expenses	14,000	
Administration	12,000	26,000
Operating Profit		14,000
Interest		3,500
Net Profit		10,500

Balance Sheet

	(€)	(€)
Fixed Assets		52,500
Current Assets	35,000	
Less Current Liabilities	17,500	
		17,500
Net Current Assets		70,000
Financed by		
Other Secured Capital	24,500	
Plus Reserves	10,500	
Equity	35,000	
10% Loans	35,000	
	70,000	

Question 3.5

E. Hand has asked you to prepare his accounts for the year ended 31 May 2002. He provides you with the following information.

1. Summary of Bank Account

	Dr (€)	Cr (€)
Balance 1 June 2001		6,200
Lodgements	360,000	
Drawings		14,500
Petty Cash		7,400
Purchases		244,000
Wages		28,600
Insurances		3,800
Light & Heat		7,600
Equipment		4,235
Motor Expenses		6,790
Tax Paid		36,750
Telephone & Postage		2,540
Deposit on Premises		8,000
Bank Interest		3,660
Balance 31 May 2002	14,075	
	374,075	374,075

2. Balances at 1 June 2001 were: Stocks €28,500; Debtors €15,600; Creditors €21,830; PAYE/PRSI €6,260 owed; Value Added Tax €2,600 owed.
3. Balances at 31 May 2002 were: Stocks €39,200; Debtors €18,600; Creditors €26,980; PAYE/PRSI €7,900 owed, Equipment 15,000.

4. Mr Hand received a loan from his brother for €8,000 during the year. No repayments were made and no interest is payable.
5. Motor car cost €15,000 on 1 June 2000.
6. Equipment cost €12,000 on 1 June 2000. One item costing €2,000 was traded against new equipment at a value of €1,500 on 01/06/2001.
7. The balance of the cost of the premises €75,000 was funded by a bank loan, repayable over ten years. No repayments were made before 31 May 2002. Interest accrued on 31 May 2002 was €3,750.
8. Part of the premises was let on 1 March 2002 for €2,400 per annum, payable in advance.
9. Analysis of tax paid is as follows.

	(€)
Personal Income Tax	7,500
PAYE/PRSI	12,200
Value Added Tax	17,050
	36,750

10. Summary of Value Added Tax Returns is as follows.

	(€)	(€)
VAT on Sales		41,500
VAT on Purchases	22,200	
VAT on Equipment	735	22,935
VAT Payable		18,565

11. Analysis of Petty Cash is as follows.

	(€)
Drawings	2,400
Motor Expenses	3,600
Miscellaneous	1,400
	7,400

12. Depreciation is to be provided on cost of fixed assets held at the year end as follows: Motor Vehicles 20% per annum; Equipment 10% per annum.
13. All receipts were lodged and the balance of lodgements was from sales.

Prepare

(a) Trading and Profit & Loss Accounts for the year ended 31 May 2002 and a
(b) Balance Sheet at 31 May 2002.

Solution to Q 3.5(a)

E. Hand
Trading and Profit & Loss Accounts for Year Ended 31 May 2002

	(€)	(€)
Sales		311,100
Stocks (1/6/2001)	28,500	
Purchases	226,950	
	255,450	
Stocks (31/5/2002)	39,200	
Cost of Sales		216,250
Gross Profit		94,850
Rent Receivable		600
		95,450
Expenses		
Wages	42,440	
Insurances	3,800	
Light & Heat	7,600	
Motor Expenses	10,390	
Telephone & Postage	2,540	
Bank Interest	7,410	
Miscellaneous	1,400	
Loss on Sale of Equipment	300	
Depreciation	4,500	
		80,380
Net Profit		15,070

Solution to Q 3.5(b)

E Hand
Balance Sheet at 31 May 2002

	Cost (€)	Depreciation (€)	Book Value (€)
Fixed Assets			
Premises	83,000		83,000
Motor Vehicles	15,000	6,000	9,000
Equipment	15,000	2,500	12,500
	113,000	8,500	104,500
Current Assets			
Stocks		39,200	
Debtors		18,600	
		57,800	
Current Liabilities			
Bank	14,075		
Creditors	26,980		
Loan from Brother	8,000		
Accrued Expenses	17,565	66,620	
			8,820
			95,680

Continued

E Hand *Continued*

	Cost (€)	Depreciation (€)	Book Value (€)
Non-Current Liabilities			
Bank Loan			75,000
			20,680
Capital Account			
Balance (1/6/2001)			30,010
Add Net Profit			15,070
			45,080
Less Drawings			24,400
Balance (31/5/2002)			20,680

Workings

Opening Capital

	(€)	(€)
Assets		
Motor Vehicle (€15,000 – €3,000)		12,000
Equipment (€12,000 – €1,200)		10,800
Stocks	28,500	
Debtors	15,600	
		66,900
Liabilities		
Bank	6,200	
Creditors	21,830	
PAYE/PRSI	6,260	
Value Added Tax	2,600	
		36,980
		30,010

Sales Receipts

	(€)	(€)
Lodgements		360,000
Less Loan from Brother	8,000	
Less Rent received	2,400	10,400
		349,600

Accrued Expenses

	(€)
PAYE/PRSI	7,900
Rent Rec. prepaid	1,800
Int	3,750
VAT due	4,115
	17,565

Workings:

Debtors Control a/c

Balance	15,600	Bank	349,600
*Sales Figures	352,600	Balance	18,600
	€378,600		€378,600

*352,600 is inclusive of VAT
Sales = 352,600 – 41,500 = 311,100

Creditors Control a/c

Bank	244,000	Balance	21,830
Balance	26,980	*Purchases	249,150
	€270,980		€270,980

*249,150 is inclusive of VAT
Purchases = 249,150 – 22,200
= 226,950

VAT

1/6/2001	Due	(2,600)
	Paid	17,050
Charge for year		18,565
31/5/2002	Due	4,115

PAYE/PRSI

1/6/2001	Due	(6,260)
	Paid	12,200
31/5/2002	Due	7,900
For year		13,840

Wages = 28,600 + 13,840 = 42,440

Question 3.6

James Burke completed his first year's trading on 31 March 2001 and has asked you to prepare his final accounts. He has not, however, kept full records. The following information is available.

1. Summary of Bank Account

	Dr (€)	Cr (€)
Opening Balance		7,250
Lodgement	392,000	
Purchases		301,000
Motor Expenses		3,700
Wages		28,400
Light & Heat		940
Petty Cash		4,900
Telephone & Postage		1,150
Drawings		8,750
Tax Paid		28,800
Rent		6,000
Balance		1,110
	392,000	392,000

2. Stock at 1 April 2000 had cost €12,200 of which €8,400 had been paid for at that date.
3. The premises was rented for €500 per month from 31 March 2000, two months' rent payable in advance.
4. Equipment bought on 31 March 2000 cost €3,000. Depreciation is at 10 per cent per annum.
5. Motor car bought and paid for in March 2000 cost €12,000. Depreciation is at 20 per cent per annum.

6. A bad debt of €500 was written off during the year.
7. Balances at 31 March 2001 were: Stocks €9,400; Debtors €6,450; Creditors €12,100; PAYE/PRSI €1,400.
8. Petty Cash analysis is as follows: Drawings €2,600; Repairs & Renewals €1,500; Miscellaneous €800.
9. Analysis of Tax Paid is as follows: Income Tax €8,000; PAYE/PRSI €9,100; Value Added Tax €11,700.
10. Summary of Value Added Tax Return is as follows: VAT on Sales €52,600; VAT on Purchases €39,100; VAT Payable €13,500.
11. Value Added Tax refunded in the year was €750.
12. Part of the premises was sublet during the year, and rent received was €3,600.
13. All receipts were lodged, and apart from items referred to above, the balance of lodgements was from sales.

Prepare final accounts for the year ended 31 March 2001 and a balance sheet at 31 March 2001.

Solution to Q 3.6

James Burke
Trading and Profit & Loss Accounts for Year Ended 31 March 2001

	(€)	(€)
Sales		341,500
Stocks (1/4/2000)	12,200	
Purchases	270,200	
	282,400	
Stocks (31/3/2001)	9,400	
Cost of Sales		273,000
Gross Profit		68,500
Rent Received		3,600
		72,100
Expenses		
Motor Expenses	3,700	
Wages	38,900	
Light & Heat	940	
Telephone & Postage	1,150	
Rent	6,000	
Repairs & Renewals	1,500	
Miscellaneous Expenses	800	
Bad Debt	500	
Depreciation	2,700	
		56,190
Net Profit		15,910

Workings

	(€)
Lodgement	392,000
Tax Refund	(750)
Rent	(3,600)
Sales	387,650

Debtors Control

Bal	—	Bank	387,650
Sales	394,100	Bal.	6,450
	394,100		394,100

394,100 includes VAT of 52,600

Sales excl. VAT 341,500

Wages	28,400
RAYE/PRSI	9,100
	+ 1,400
	38,900

James Burke
Balance Sheet at 31 March 2001

	Cost (€)	Depreciation (€)	Book Value (€)
Fixed Assets			
Motor Car	12,000	2,400	9,600
Equipment	3,000	300	2,700
	15,000	2,700	12,300
Current Assets			
Stock		9,400	
Debtors		6,450	
Rent Prepaid		1,000	
Bank		1,110	
		17,960	
Current Liabilities			
Creditors	12,100		
PAYE/PRSI	1,400		
Value Added Tax	2,550		
		16,050	
Net Current Assets			1,910
			14,210
Capital Account			
Balance (1/4/2000)			17,650
Add Net Profit			15,910
			33,560
Less Drawings		11,350	
Less Income Tax Paid		8,000	
			19,350
Balance (31/3/2001)			14,210

Question 3.7

V. Goode purchased a business on 1 January 2001 for €98,000 consisting of Shop Premises €84,000; Stock €11,000; Debtors €9,000; Creditors €12,000; Business Rates Prepaid for three months €900; Light & Heat due €1,500.

During the year he did not keep a full set of accounts but was able to supply the following information on 31 December 2001.

1. On 1 June 2001 Goode borrowed €54,000 from International Finance Limited, some of which was used to purchase an adjoining premises for €50,000. The rate of interest was 12 per cent per annum payable monthly at the end of each month. The capital sum was to be repaid in one lump sum in 2015, and to provide for this, the bank was to transfer €180 per month into an investment fund.

2. Each week Goode took from stock goods valued at €70 and cash of €90 for private expenses.
3. Goode received a legacy of €30,000 and invested two-thirds of this in the business.
4. The following payments were made from the business bank account: Rates for twelve months €4,200; Interest €3,240; College Fees €4,500; Wages and General Expenses €29,700; Light & Heat €7,500; Motor Vehicles €24,000.
5. Goode estimated that one-quarter of Interest Payable and Light & Heat used should be attributed to the private section of the business. Included in Motor Vehicles is a car bought for his daughter valued at €8,000. Half of the College Fees were for business courses attended by employees and the remainder for family members.
6. Included in the assets and liabilities of the firm on 31 December 2001 were: Stock €14,500; Debtors €11,200; Creditors €13,300; Bank €15,000; Electricity due €600; €60 interest earned by the fund to date.
7. No provision has yet been made for depreciation of premises of 1 per cent per annum and depreciation on Motor Vehicles at 20 per cent, a full years depreciation to apply to all fixed assets.
8. Goode's Gross Profit was $33\frac{1}{3}$ per cent of Sales.

Prepare

(a) Trading and Profit & Loss Accounts and
(b) a Balance Sheet, and
(c) Advise V. Goode.

Solution to Q 3.7

General Journal

	DR (€)	CR (€)
Capital		98,000
Shop Premises	84,000	
Opening Stock	11,000	
Debtors	9,000	
Creditors		12,000
Rates (3 months)	900	
Light & Heat		1,500
Goodwill	6,600	
	111,500	111,500

Loan interest = $54{,}000 \times 12\% \times 7/12 = 3{,}780$
Investment Fund = $(180 \times 7) + 60$

Rates Account

Balance	900	Profit & Loss	4,050
Bank	4,200	Balance	1,050
	5,100		5,100

Interest Account

Bank	3,240	Drawings	945
Balance	540	Profit & Loss	2,835
	3,780		3,780

Light & Heat Account

Bank	7,500	Balance	1,500
Balance	600	Drawings	1,650
		Profit & Loss	4,950
	8,100		8,100

Drawings

Purchases	3,640		
Cash	4,680		
College Fees	2,250		
Interest	945		
Light & Heat	1,650		
Motor Vehicles	8,000		
	21,165		

Trading and Profit & Loss Accounts for the Year Ended 31/12/2001

	(€)	(€)	
Sales		224,760	B
Opening Stock	11,000		
Purchases (156,980 – 3,640)	153,340		
	164,340		
Less Closing Stock	14,500		
Cost of Sales		149,840	A
Gross Profit		74,920	
Rates	4,050		
Light & Heat	4,950		
Interest	2,835		
Depreciation: Premises	1,340		
Wages & General Expenses (29,700 + 2,250)	31,950	45,125	
		29,795	
Plus Investment Income		60	
Net Profit		29,855	X

Total of Expenses

X = N. Profit from the Balance sheet
29,855 – Gain €60 + Expenses 45,125 = Gross Profit
Gross Profit × 3 = Sales (B)
Gross Profit × 2 = Cost of Sales (A)

Balance Sheet at 31 December 2001

	(€)	(€)	(€)
Fixed Assets			
Shop Premises (134,000 – 1%) (84,000 + 50,000)			132,660
Motor Vehicles (24,000 – 8,000 – 20%)			12,800
			145,460
Goodwill		6,600	
Investment Fund		1,320	7,920
			153,380
Current Assets			
Stock	14,500		
Debtors	11,200		
Bank	15,000		
Rates Prepaid	1,050	41,750	
Less Current Liabilities			
Creditors	13,300		
Electricity Due	600		
Interest Due	540	14,440	
			27,310
			180,690
Financed by			
Capital (98,000 + 20,000)	118,000		
Plus Net Profit * (missing figure)	29,855		
Less Drawings	(21,165)		
Loan	54,000		
			180,690

Question 3.8
On 1 January 2000 J. Perry purchased a business for €90,000 consisting of Premises €85,000; Stock €14,200; Building Insurance Prepaid €800; Trade Creditors €9,400; Electricity due €600. During the year Perry did not keep a full set of books but was able to supply the following information on 31 December 2000. Cash Payments: General Expenses €24,200; Lodgements €44,000; Purchases €31,800; Light & Heat €4,800. Bank Payments: Creditors €19,800; Insurance €3,300; Family Holiday €2,700; Delivery Vans €24,000; Interest €2,400. Bank Lodgements: Cash €44,000; Debtors €21,200; Capital €10,000.

During the year Perry took from stock goods to the value of €60 per week and €40 cash per week for household expenses.

On 1 August 2000 Perry had borrowed €60,000, part of which was used to purchase an adjoining building costing €55,000. The rate of interest on this loan was 12 per cent per annum payable monthly on the last day of the month. The capital sum was to be repaid in one lump sum in 2010, and to provide for this, Perry signed a standing order for the transfer of €400 per month into an investment account commencing on 1 September 2000 (ignore investment income). Perry estimated that one-fifth of Light & Heat used and Insurance paid during the year should be attributed to the private section of the premises. Included in the assets and liabilities of the firm on 31 December 2000 were Debtors €22,400; Trade Creditors €18,700; Stock €15,900; Cash €400; Insurance Prepaid €900; Electricity due €300.

You are required to show, with workings,

(a) Trading and Profit & Loss Accounts for the year ended 31 December 2000 and a
(b) Balance Sheet at 31 December 2000.

Solution to Q 3.8

J. Perry
Trading and Profit & Loss Accounts for the Year Ended 31 December 2000

	(€)	(€)
Sales		150,880
Less Cost of Sales		
Stock (1/1/2000)	14,200	
Add Purchases	*57,780	
	71,980	
Less Stock (31/12/2000)	15,900	56,080
		94,800
Less Expenses		
General Expenses	24,200	
Insurance	2,540	
Interest	3,000	
Light & Heat	3,600	33,340
Net Profit		€61,460

*Purch. = 57,780 + drawings 3,120 = 60,900

Balance Sheet at 31 December 2000

	(€)	(€)	(€)
Fixed Assets			
Buildings			140,000
Delivery Vans			24,000
			164,000
Investments			1,600
			165,600
Current Assets			
Stock		15,900	
Debtors		22,400	
Cash		400	
Bank		26,400	
Insurance Prepaid		900	
		66,000	
Less Current Liabilities			
Creditors	18,700		
Electricity Due	300		
Interest Due	600	19,600	46,400
			212,000
Financed by			
Capital (1/1/2000)		90,000	
Add Capital Introduced		10,000	
Add Net Profit		61,460	
Less Drawings		9,460	152,000
Long-Term Liabilities			
Loan			60,000
			212,000

Chapter 4

Club Accounts

Remember

Accumulated Fund = Capital.

Excess of Income over Expenditure = Profit.

Excess of Expenditure over Income = Loss.

Life Membership = Reserve.

Levy Reserve Fund = Reserve.

In doing the questions in this chapter, follow these steps.

1. Enter the Accumulated Fund figures in a general journal format but do not add them, as they are usually not complete.
2. Lay out a blank Bar Trading Account and fill in the figures as you find them. Remember that

   Sales = Receipts – Opening Debtors + Closing Debtors

   Stock figures are as given

   Purchases = Payments to Creditors – Opening Creditors + Closing Creditors
3. Lay out the Income & Expenditure Account on a separate page.

   Subscriptions = Receipts + Prepaid at Beginning of Year + Due at End of Year – due at Beginning of Year (last year's) – Prepaid at End of Year (next year's).

   Set off linked items to show a Profit/Loss for the item, e.g. Catering Receipts – Catering Expenses to show a Catering Profit/Loss. In calculating Loan interest, only allocate to the Income & Expenditure that portion paid or payable for the year. The previous interest was a liability at the beginning of the year and goes back into the Accumulated Fund calculation.
4. In the Balance Sheet, do not omit items such as Depreciation, Investments, Subscriptions Due/Prepaid. Again remember that Life Membership and Levy Reserve are actually Reserves.
5. Do not omit section (d) where you are asked to advise the Club on its financial policy. You are only asked for a brief answer, but a large number of students omit it altogether.

Question 4.1

Included in the assets and liabilities of the LOVE All Tennis Club on 1 January 2001 were the following: Clubhouse and Land €190,000; Equipment at Cost €7,500; Bar Stock €8,000; Subscriptions in Advance €500; Bar Debtors €350; Bar Creditors €3,200; Affiliation Fees due €300.

The club treasurer has supplied the following account of the club's activities for the year ended 31 December 2001.

Receipts	(€)	Payments	(€)
Bank Current Account	10,000	Sundry Expenses	14,500
Bar Receipts	78,000	Bar Purchases	57,000
Subscriptions	43,500	Affiliation Fees	900
Disposal of Equipment (cost €2,000)	800	Competition Prizes	1,100
Interest from 6% Government		Catering costs	3,100
Investment of €15,000	1,350	Purchase of 7% Government	
Catering Receipts	4,600	Bonds on 31 August 2001	12,000
Competition Receipts	600	Transfer to Deposit Account	
		on 31 December 2001	10,000
		Purchase of Prize Bonds	200
		Repayment of €14,000 Loan	
		on 30 June 2001 with	
		1.5 year's interest	16,520
		Balance	23,530
	138,850		138,850

You are given the following additional information:

1. Bar Stock on 31 December 2001 is €8,800.
2. Subscriptions include three life memberships of €800 each, and there are subscriptions due of €500.
3. Equipment at 31 December 2001 is to be depreciation at the rate of 20 per cent per annum.
4. Bar Debtors and Creditors are €360 and €3,400, respectively.
5. Life Membership is to be credited to Income over a five-year period beginning in 2001.

Prepare the following:

(a) a Statement of Accumulated Fund at 1 January 2001,
(b) an Income & Expenditure Account for the year ended 31 December 2001,
(c) a Balance Sheet at 31 December 2001 and
(d) a report to the members on the advisability of purchasing a piece of land adjoining their property that has come on the market at €200,000.

Solution to Q 4.1(a)

The LOVE ALL Tennis Club
Accumulated Fund on 1 January 2001

	Dr (€)	Cr (€)
Clubhouse & Land	190,000	
Equipment	7,500	
Bar Stock	8,000	
Subscriptions in Advance		500
Bar Debtors	350	
Bar Creditors		3,200
Affiliation Fees Due		300
Bank	10,000	
6% Government Investment	15,000	
6% Investment Income Due	450	
Loan		14,000
Interest Due		1,680
Accumulated Fund		211,620
	231,300	231,300

Solution to Q 4.1(b)

Income & Expenditure Account for the Year Ended 31 December 2001

	Workings*		(€)
Income			
Bar Profit	W1	21,610	
Subscriptions	W2	42,100	
Catering Profit (4,600 – 3,100)		1,500	
6% Investment Income		900	
7% Investment Income		280	
Life Membership		480	66,870
Expenditure			
Sundry Expenses		14,500	
Affiliation Fees (900 – 300)		600	
Loss on Competitions (1,100 – 600)		500	
Interest		840	
Loss on Disposal of Equipment		1,200	
Depreciation of Equipment		1,100	18,740
Excess of Income			48,130

Workings

W1

Bar Trading Account

		(€)
Sales (78,000 – 350 + 360)		78,010
Less Cost of Opening Stock	8,000	
Add Purchases (57,000 – 3,200 + 3,400)	57,200	
	65,200	
Less Closing Stock	8,800	
Cost		56,400
Gross Profit		21,610

W2 Subscriptions 43,500 + 500 – 2,400 + 500 = 42,100

	(€)
Life Membership	2,400
Income	480
Reserves	1,920

Solution to Q 4.1(c)

Balance Sheet at 31 December 2001

	Cost (€)	Accumulated Depreciation (€)	Net (€)
Fixed Assets			
Clubhouse & Land	190,000		190,000
Equipment	5,500	1,100	4,400
	195,500	1,100	194,400
6% Government Stock			15,000
Prize Bonds			200
7% Government Bonds			12,000
			221,600

Continued

Balance Sheet at 31 December 2001 *Continued*

	Cost (€)	Accumulated Depreciation (€)	Net (€)
Current Assets			
Bank	23,530		
Closing Stock	8,800		
Bar Debtors	360		
Deposit Account	10,000		
Subscriptions Due	500		
Income Due on 7% Bond	280		
	43,470		
Less Current Liabilities/Creditors	3,400		40,070
			261,670
Financed by			
Accumulated Fund	211,620		
Excess of Income	48,130		
Life Membership	1,920		
			261,670

Solution to Q 4.1(d)

Points in favour of purchase:

The Club has liquid assets of Government Investments €27,000; Deposit Account €10,000; Current Account €23,530. In addition,

- It has repaid its loan.
- It could levy its members.
- It could offer reduced Life Membership (which might reduce its future income).
- It could apply for lottery funding.
- It could finance some borrowing.

Points against purchase:

- The land might not be suitable for development.
- There may be planning permission problems.
- Development costs may be very high.
- The club may have a burden of interest/loan repayments in the future.

Question 4.2

Included in the assets and liabilities of the Below-Par Golf Club at 1 January 2002 were the following: Clubhouse & Land €180,000; Life Membership €18,000; Equipment at Book Value €17,000; Bar Debtors €250; Bar Creditors €5,600; Levy Reserve Fund €40,000; Bar Stock €6,600.

The club treasurer has supplied the following information regarding the club's activities during the year ended 31 December 2002.

	Receipts (€)	Payments (€)	
Bank Current Account	12,000	Catering Expenses	3,400
Interest from 7% Government Investments 2001	2,100	Sundry Expenses	24,000
Interest from 7% Government Investments 2002	2,100	Greenkeepers' Wages	15,900
Catering Receipts	5,800	Bar Purchases	56,750
Bar Receipts	84,600	Repayment of €30,000 loan on 30 September 02 with $2\frac{1}{2}$ years' interest	38,000
Subscriptions	96,300	Equipment	9,000
		Transfer to Deposit Account on 31 December 02	20,000
		Balance	35,850
	202,900		202,900

You are given the following additional information.

1. Bar Stock is €6,900.
2. Equipment owed at 31 December 2002 is valued at €23,500.
3. Subscriptions include the following; two life memberships, which brings the total to fourteen, a levy for the year of €50 on 400 members and a levy of €50 on ten members which has been pending since last year.
4. Debtors and Creditors are €300 and €5,500, respectively.
5. Greenkeepers' wages due are €1,400.

Prepare the following:

(a) a Statement of Accumulated Fund at 1 January 2002,
(b) an Income & Expenditure Account for the year ended 31 December 2002,
(c) a Balance Sheet at 31 December 2002 and
(d) a report to the members on funding €100,000 extension

Solution to Q 4.2(a)

Below Par Golf Club
Accumulated Fund on 1 January 2002

	Workings	Dr (€)	Cr (€)
Clubhouse & Land		180,000	
Life Membership			18,000
Equipment (net)		1,700	
Bar Debtors		250	
Bar Creditors			5,600
Levy Reserve Fund			40,000
Bar Stock		6,600	
Bank		12,000	
7% Investments		30,000	
Investment Income Due		2,100	
Levy Fund Due		500	
Loan	W3		30,000
Interest Due	W3		5,600
Accumulated Fund			149,250
		248,450	248,450

Solution to Q 4.2(b)

Income & Expenditure Account for the
Year Ended 31 December 2002

	Workings*	(€)	(€)
Income			
Bar Profit	W1	28,300	
7% Investment Income		2,100	
Catering Profit (5,800 – 3,400)		2,400	
Subscriptions	W2	72,800	105,600
Expenditure			
Sundry Expenses		24,000	
Greenkeepers' Wages (15,900 + 1,400)		17,300	
Loan Interest	W3	2,400	
Depreciation — Equipment		2,500	46,200
Excess of Income			59,400

*Workings

W1. Bar Trading Account

	(€)	(€)
Sales (84,600 – 250 + 300)		84,650
Less Cost		
Opening Stock	6,600	
Add Purchases (56,750 – 5,600 + 5,500)	56,650	
	63,250	
Less Closing Stock	6,900	
Cost of Sales		56,350
Profit		28,300

W2. Subscriptions

	(€)
Subscriptions	96,300
Life	(3,000)
Levy	(20,000)
Levy	(500)
	72,800

W3. Loan

	(€)
Repaid	38,000
Loan	30,000
Total Interest	8,000
$\frac{1}{2}$ years' Interest	1,600
1 years' Interest	3,200
9 months' Interest	2,400
Interest Due	5,600

Solution to Q 4.2(c)

Balance Sheet at 31 December 2002

	Cost (€)	Account Depreciation (€)	Net (€)
Fixed Assets			
Clubhouse & Land	180,000		180,000
Equipment	26,000	2,500	23,500
	206,000	2,500	203,500
7% Investments (or C/A)			30,000
Current Assets			
Stock	6,900		
Debtors	300		
Bank	35,850		
Deposit Account	20,000		
		63,050	
Less Current Liabilities			
Creditors	5,500		
Greenkeepers' Wages	1,400	6,900	56,150
			289,650
Enhanced By			
Accumulated Fund			149,250
Excess of Income			59,400
Levy Reserve Fund			60,000
Life Membership			21,000
			289,650

Solution to Q 4.2(d) Funding Extension €100,000

Don't wait two years
Why
35,850 in Current Account
20,000 in Deposit Account
30,000 in Investment Fund
Loan paid off
Lottery funding?

Question 4.3

Included in the assets and liabilities of the Nokemdown Indoor and Outdoor Bowling Club on 1 January 2001 were the following: Clubhouse & Land €285,000; Equipment €28,000; Bar Stock €16,000; Life Membership €30,000; Bar Debtors €130; Bar Creditors €4,300; Levy Reserve Fund €16,000; 6 per cent Investment Income due €300; Wages due €200.

The club treasurer has supplied the following information for the year ended 31 December 2001.

Receipts	(€)	Payments	(€)
Catering Receipts	7,600	Bar Current Account	4,560
Annual Grant	5,500	Equipment	9,000
Subscriptions	53,200	Catering Costs	8,300
Interest from 6% Investments	1,800	Wages	15,200
Bar Receipts	72,600	General Expenses	24,000
Sale of Equipment	1,600	Bar Purchases	61,000
		Repayment of €16,000 Loan on 30 September 2001 with $2\frac{1}{4}$ years' interest	19,600
		Balance	540
	142,200		142,200

You are also given the following information.

1. Bar Stock on 31 December 2001 is €16,500.
2. Subscriptions include the following:
   (i) Three Life Memberships bringing the total to sixty-three.
   (ii) Levy for 2001 is 400 members at €40.
   (iii) Levy from five members for 2000.
   (iv) Subscriptions due 400.
3. Bar Debtors and Creditors are €150 and €4,800 respectively.
4. Book value of Equipment €31,000.

Prepare the following:

1. a Statement of Accumulated Fund at 1 January 2001,
2. an Income and Expenditure Account for the year ended 31 December 2001,
3. a Balance Sheet at 31 December 2001 and
4. a report to the Club on their financial position.

Solution to Q 4.3(a)

Nokemdown Indoor and Outdoor Bowling Club
Accumulated Fund 1 January 2001

	Dr (€)	Cr (€)
Clubhouse & Land	285,000	
Equipment	28,000	
Bar Stock	16,000	
Life Membership		30,000
Bar Debtors	130	
Bar Creditors		4,300
Levy Reserve Fund		16,000
Investment Income Due	300	
Wages Due		200
Bank		4,560
6% Investments	25,000	
Levy Fund Due	200	
Loan		16,000
Interest Due		2,400
Accumulated Fund		281,170
	354,630	354,630

* Workings

W1.

Subscriptions

	(€)
Subscriptions	53,200
Life Membership	(1,500)
Levy 2001	(16,000)
Levy 2000	(200)
Due	400
	35,900

W2.

Bar Trading Account

		(€)
Sales (72,600 – 130 + 150)		72,620
Less Cost Opening Stock	16,000	
Purchases (61,000 – 4,300 + 4,800)	61,500	
	77,500	
Less Closing Stock	16,500	
Cost of Sales		61,000
Profit		11,620

Solution to Q 4.3(b)

Income & Expenditure Account for the Year Ended 31 December 2001

	Workings*	(€)	(€)
Income			
Annual Grant		5,500	
Subscriptions	W1	35,900	
Investment Income		1,500	
Bar Profit	W2	11,620	54,520
Expenditure			
Catering Loss (8,300 – 7,500)		800	
Wages (15,200 – 200)		15,000	
General Expenses		24,000	
Loan Interest		1,200	
Depreciation — Equipment	W3	4,400	45,400
Excess of Income			9,120

W3. Equipment Depreciation

Equipment (28,000 – 1,600 + 900) =	35,400
Value 31 December 2001 =	31,000
Depreciation =	4,400

Solution Q 4.3(c)

Balance Sheet at 31 December 2001

	Cost (€)	Accumulated Depreciation (€)	Net (€)
Fixed Assets			
Clubhouse & Land	285,000		285,000
Equipment	35,400	4,400	31,000
	320,400	4,400	316,000
Current Assets			
Bar Stock	16,500		
Bar Debtors	150		
Bank	540		
6% Investments	25,00		
Subs due	400		
	42,590		
Less Current Liabilities			
Creditors	4,800		
Net Current Assets			37,790
			353,790
Financed by			
Accumulated Fund *	281,170		
Excess of Income	9,120		
Levy Reserve Fund	32,000		
Life Membership	31,500		
			353,790

Solution to Q 4.3(d) Advice to Club (3 or 4 points)

Question 4.4

You are the treasurer of Crookstown Golf Club and have prepared the following receipts and payments account for the year ended 31 December 2000.

Receipts	(€)	(€)	Payments	(€)	(€)
Balance Forward:			Balance forward:		
Cash on Hand		75	Bank Account		1,200
Membership Subscriptions			Wages and Salaries		
Ordinary Members	11,000		Restaurant Staff	3,800	
Associate Members	1,600		Other Staff	8,300	
Life members	800	13,400			
				12,100	
Restaurant Receipts		13,800	Restaurant Purchases		8,600
Donations Received	950		Rent & Rates		1,600
Deposit Account	1,220		Light & Heat		1,800
			New Computer		1,600
			Restaurant Expenses		750
			Bank Interest		240
			Deposit Account		1,200
			Balance forward		
			Bank Account	315	
			Cash on Hand	40	355
		29,445			29,445
Balance forward					
Bank Account	315				
Cash on Hand	40	355			

As Treasurer, you have been asked by the club's Management Committee to prepare additional financial statements (as set out in the requirement below) and you have been supplied with the following information:

1. The clubhouse should be valued at €18,000 at 31 December 1999 and at 31 December 2000.
2. All club equipment was valued at €10,400 at 31 December 1999. Depreciation should be charged at 20 per cent on the book value of all equipment held at the club's year end.
3. Other assets and liabilities of the club are as follows:

	31 December 2000 (€)	31 December 1999 (€)
Subscriptions Due	400	Nil
Rates Prepaid	320	200
Light & Heat Unpaid (accrued)	310	250
Restaurant Creditors	1,400	1,600
Restaurant Stocks	930	850

4. Life subscriptions received are credited to a life subscriptions fund and written off to income over a ten-year period commencing in the year of receipt. The life subscriptions fund account balance on 1 January 2000 was €900, being in respect of €1,000 of life subscriptions received in the year ended 31 December 1999.
5. All subscriptions received from ordinary and associate members during 2000 were for the year ended 31 December 2000.
6. One-half of the charges for Rent & Rates and Light & Heat are in respect of the restaurant.
7. The amount of €1,200 was placed on deposit during the year and withdrawn, with interest earned, before the year end.

You are required to prepare

(a) a Statement of Affairs (Opening Balance Sheet) at 31 December 1999,
(b) a Restaurant Trading Account for the year ended 31 December 2000,
(c) an Income and Expenditure Account for the year ended 31 December 2000 and
(d) a Balance Sheet at that date.

Solution to Q 4.4(a)

Statement of Affairs of Crookstown Golf Club at 31 December 1999

	(€)	(€)	(€)
Fixed Assets			
Clubhouse			18,000
Equipment			10,400
			28,400
Current Assets			
Rates Prepaid		200	
Restaurant Stocks		850	
Cash on Hand		75	
		1,125	
Current Liabilities			
Light & Heat	250		
Restaurant Creditors	1,600		
Bank Overdraft	1,200	3,050	
Net Current Liabilities			(1,925)
			26,475
Accumulated Fund (balancing figure)			25,575
Life Members' Fund			900
			26,475

Solution to Q 4.4(b)

Restaurant Trading Account of Crookstown Golf Club for the Year Ended 31 December 2000

	(€)	(€)
Sales		13,800
Opening Stock	850	
Purchases (8,600 – 1,600 + 1,400)	8,400	
	9,250	
Closing Stock	930	8,320
Gross Profit		5,480
Less Expenses		
Wages & Salaries	3,800	
Rent & Rates [(1,600 + 200 – 320) × 50%]	740	
Light & Heat [(1,800 – 250 + 310) × 50%]	930	
Restaurant Expenses	750	6,220
Net Loss for the Year		740

Solution for Q 4.4(c)

Income & Expenditure Account of Crookstown Golf Club for the Year Ended 31 December 2000

	(€)	(€)
Income		
Subscriptions		13,180
Donations		950
Deposit Interest (1,220 – 1,200)		20
		14,150
Expenditure		
Loss on Restaurant	740	
Wages & Salaries	8,300	
Rent & Rates [(1,600 + 200 – 320) × 50%)]	740	
Light & Heat [(1,800 – 250 + 310) × 50%]	930	
Bank Interest	240	
Depreciation [(10,400 + 1,600) × 20%]	2,400	13,350
Excess of Income over Expenditure		800

Solution to Q 4.4(d)

Balance Sheet of Crookstown Golf Club at 31 December 2000

	(€)	(€)	(€)
Fixed Assets			
Clubhouse			18,000
Equipment (10,400 + 1,600 – 2,400)			9,600
			27,600
Current Assets			
Restaurant Stocks		930	
Rates Prepaid		320	
Subscription Due		400	
Bank		315	
Cash on Hand		40	
		2,005	
Current Liabilities			
Restaurant Creditors	1,400		
Light & Heat Accrual	310	1,710	
Net current assets			295
			27,895
Accumulated fund			25,575
Surplus on Income over Expenditure			800
			26,375
Life Members' Fund (900 + 800 – 180)	1,520		
			27,895

Chapter 5

Correction of Errors and Suspense Accounts

Correction of Errors and Suspense Accounts are regarded as the most difficult topic on the course. A good knowledge of basic bookkeeping is essential. All the questions require very careful reading and should never be rushed. You should use T Accounts to record what actually happened and what should have been entered, and you should then compare this to what has been entered. The real key to success is plenty of practice, but the following basic hints will be helpful.

1. When doing the journal entries, never just enter a single entry. Always complete the double entry.
2. Always write the narration under each entry.
3. As you go down through the journal entries, indicate beside each whether it is to go into the Profit & Loss Account or the Balance Sheet.
4. In writing up the Suspense Account, simply follow your own instructions; i.e. where you indicated debit in the journal entry, do the same in the suspense and likewise with the credits.
5. In amending the Profit & Loss Account, the debit items in the journal will be minuses and the credit items will be pluses.
6. In amending the Balance Sheet, debits on assets will be pluses, debits on liabilities minuses and vice versa with credits. Where you have, for example, a debit with a person's name, determine whether you are increasing a debtor or decreasing a creditor.

Question 5.1
The Trial Balance of J. Nolan, a clothes shop owner, failed to agree, and the difference was placed in the Suspense Account. The following Balance Sheet was then prepared.

Balance Sheet at 31 December 2001

	(€)	(€)	(€)
Fixed Assets			
Premises		80,000	
Furniture & Equipment		60,000	140,000
Current Assets			
Stock (including suspense)		35,000	
Debtors		12,000	
		47,000	
Less Current Liabilities			
Creditors	15,000		
Bank	7,000	22,000	
Net Current Assets			25,000
			165,000
Financed by			
Capital	125,000		
Plus Net Profit	60,000		
	185,000		
Less Drawings	20,000	165,000	

When the books were checked the following errors were discovered.

1. A private debt of €1,200 owed to Nolan had been offset in full against a business debt of €1,400 owed by Nolan.
2. Furniture sold on credit to P. Dolan for €2,760 had been entered in both the Sales Account and the wrong side of Dolan's Account as €2,670.
3. A credit note received from a creditor for €456 had been entered in the Purchases Returns Account as €465 and on the wrong side of the creditor's account as €546.
4. Goods previously sold to a debtor for €760 had been returned and entered in the books as €670. Subsequently Nolan decided to apply a restocking charge of 10 per cent of this amount, and credited the debtor with €603. No other entry had been made in the books in respect of the restocking charge.
5. Payments from the business bank account of €300 for private repairs and €250 for equipment repairs had been credited to Creditors and Equipment, respectively.

You are required to

(a) journalise the necessary corrections,
(b) show the Suspense Account,
(c) prepare a Statement showing the correct net profit and
(d) prepare the Corrected Balance Sheet.

Solution to Q 5.1(a)

J. Nolan

	Entry	Debit (€)	Credit (€)
Creditor (i)	b	1,400	
Capital	b		1,200
Discount Received	p		200

Private debt used to offset business debt of €1,400.

	Entry	Dr (€)	Cr (€)
Sales (ii)	p	2,670	
P. Dolan (debtor)	b	5,430	
Furniture	b		2,760
Suspense			5,340

Disposal of furniture entered as Sales and on wrong side of Dolan's account.

	Entry	Dr (€)	Cr (€)
Creditors (iii)	b	1,002	
Purchases Returns	p	9	
Suspense			1,011

Wrong figure for credit note entered in accounts.

	Entry	Dr (€)	Cr (€)
Debtor (iv)	b	589	
Sales Returns	p	14	
Suspense			603

	Entry	Dr (€)	Cr (€)
Drawings (v)	b	300	
Equipment Repairs	p	250	
Creditors	b	300	
Equipment	b	250	
Suspense			1,100

Solution to Q 5.1(b)

Suspense Account

	(€)		(€)
Difference	8,054	(ii) Sales, etc	5,340
		(iii) Creditors, etc	1,011
		(iv) Debtors, etc	603
		(v) Drawings, etc	1,100
	8,054		8,054

Solution to Q 5.1(c)

Amended Net Profit

	Minus (€)	Plus (€)	(€)
Net Profit per Accounts			60,000
Discount Received		200	
Sales	(2,670)		
Purchases Returns	(9)		
Sales Returns	(14)		
Repairs	(250)		
	(2,943)	200	(2,743)
Corrected Profit			57,257

Solution to Q 5.1(d)

Corrected Balance Sheet

		(€)	(€)
Fixed Assets			
Premises		80,000	
Furniture & Equipment (60,000 – 2,760 + 250)		57,490	
			137,490
Current Assets			
Stock (35,000 – 8,054)		26,946	
Debtors (12,000 + 5,430 + 589)		18,019	
		44,965	
Less Current Liabilities			
Creditors (15,000 – 1,400 – 1,000 – 300)	12,298		
Bank	7,000	19,298	
Working Capital			25,667
			€163,157
Financed by			
Capital (125,000 + 1,200)			126,200
Add Net Profit			57,257
			183,457
Less Drawings (20,000 + 300)			(20,300)
			163,157

Question 5.2

The Trial Balance of R. Gillen, a grocer, failed to agree on 31 December 2000. The difference was entered in the Suspense Account, and the following Balance Sheet was prepared.

Balance Sheet at 31 December 2000

	(€)	(€)	(€)
Fixed Assets			
Premises		165,000	
Fixtures & Equipment		33,000	198,000
Current Assets			
Stock		94,000	
Debtors		10,600	
Cash		400	
		105,000	

Continued

Balance Sheet at 31 December 2000 *Continued*

	(€)	(€)	(€)
Less Current Liabilities			
Creditors (incorporating suspense)	72,000		
Bank	19,000	91,000	14,000
			212,000
Financed by			
Capital		176,000	
Add Net Profit		42,000	
		218,000	
Less Drawings		6,000	212,000
			212,000

On checking the books, the following errors were revealed.

1. Gillen sent a cheque for €520 in full settlement of a business debt of €560, and this was recorded correctly in the books. However, no entry has been made in the books of the subsequent dishonouring of this cheque and the payment on account of €300 cash by Gillen.
2. Repairs to premises €600 and repairs to private dwelling house €360 were paid out of the business Bank Account and credited to Premises Account.
3. A private debt of €390 owed by Gillen to a debtor of the business had been offset in full settlement against a business debt of €400 owed to Gillen. No entry had been made in the books.
4. Gillen had given a private car, valued at €4,500 to a creditor of the business to offset, in full, a debt of €4,700. This transaction had been treated in error as a credit purchase of stock for €4,500.
5. Goods previously sold to a debtor for €530 had been returned to Gillen and entered in the books in error as €350. Subsequently, Gillen decided to apply a restocking charge of 10 per cent to these returns, and he immediately credited the debtor with €315. No other entry was made in the books in respect of the restocking charge.

Your are required to

(a) journalise the necessary corrections,
(b) show the Suspense Account,
(c) prepare a Statement showing the correct net profit and
(d) prepare the corrected Balance Sheet.

Solution to Q 5.2(a)

R. Gillen

	Dr (€)	Cr (€)
Bank Account	520	
Discount	40	
Creditors Account		260
Cash		300

Being the recording of a dishonoured cheque issued by Gillen and payment on account of €300 in cash.

	Dr (€)	Cr (€)
Premises Account	960	
Drawings Account	360	
Repairs Account	600	
Suspense Account		1,920

Being cancellation of entry in Premises Account and recording of payments in Drawings and Repairs accounts.

	Dr (€)	Cr (€)
Drawings/Capital Account	390	
Discount Account	10	
Debtors Account		400

Being a private debt of €400 owed by Gillen offset against a business debt of €530 owed to Gillen.

Discount Received Account	Dr (€)	Cr (€)

	Dr (€)	Cr (€)
Creditors Account	9,200	
Purchase Account		4,500
Discount Received Account		200
Capital Account		4,500

Being recording of €4,500 introduced as capital by Gillen and cancellation of incorrect entries in Creditors and Purchases Accounts.

	Dr (€)	Cr (€)
Debtors Account	188	
Sales Returns Account	127	
Suspense Account		315

Being the recording of restock charge and correction of incorrect entry in Sales Returns and Debtors Accounts.

Solution to Q 5.2(b)

Suspense Account

	(€)		(€)
Difference	2,235	Premises	960
		Drawings	360
		Repairs	600
		Debtors	315
	2,235		2,235

Solution to Q 5.2(c)

Statement of Corrected Net Profit

	(€)	(€)
Net Profit as per books		4,200
Add Purchases	4,500	
Discount Received	200	
		4,700
		46,700
Deduct Discount	40	
Repairs	600	
Discount	10	
Sales Returns	127	777
		45,923

Solution to Q 5.2(d)

Corrected Balance Sheet at 31 December 2000

	(€)	(€)	(€)
Fixed Assets			
Premises		165,960	
Fixtures & Equipment		33,000	198,960
Current Assets			
Stock		94,000	
Debtors		10,388	
Cash		100	
		104,488	
Less Current Liabilities			
Creditors	65,295		
Bank	18,480	83,775	20,713
			219,673
Financed by			
Capital		180,500	
Add Net Profit		45,923	
		226,423	
Less Drawings	6,750	219,673	
			219,673

Question 5.3

The Trial Balance of J. Quinlan, a garage owner, failed to agree on 31 December 2001. The difference was entered in the Suspense Account, and the following Balance Sheet was prepared.

Balance Sheet at 31 December 2001

	(€)	(€)	(€)
Fixed Assets			
Premises	120,000		
Fixtures & Equipment	40,000	160,000	
Current Assets			
Stock		140,000	
Debtors (incorporating suspense)		15,000	
		155,000	
Less Current Liabilities			
Creditors	80,000		
Bank	30,000	110,000	45,000
			205,000

Continued

Balance Sheet at 31 December 2000 *Continued*

	(€)	(€)	(€)
Financed by			
Capital		194,000	
Add Net Profit		24,000	
		218,000	
Less Drawings		13,000	205,000
			€205,000

On checking the books, the following errors and omissions were discovered.

1. A motor car, purchased on credit from J. Brady for €9,300 had been entered as €9,500 in the Furniture & Equipment Account and also as €9,500 on the incorrect side of Brady's Account.
2. A private debt of €220 owed by Quinlan to R. Murphy had been offset in full against a bill for €250 owed by Murphy for car repairs previously carried out. No entry had been made.
3. Wages due to an employee of €210 had not been entered in the books.
4. J. Quinlan won a Holiday prize for two worth €1,800. One ticket had been given to a salesman as part payment of the salesman's commission for the year and the other to a creditor as payment in full of a debt of €950. No entry had been made in the books.
5. A credit note received from a creditor for €650 had been entered correctly in the day book but posted twice to the incorrect side of the creditor's account as €560.

You are required to

(a) journalise the necessary corrections,
(b) show the Suspense Account,
(c) prepare a Statement showing the correct net profit and
(d) prepare the corrected Balance Sheet.

Solution to Q 5.3(a)

	Debit (€)	Credit (€)
Purchases Account	9,300	
Suspense Account	19,000	
J. Brady Account		18,800
Furniture & Equipment Account		9,500

Being stock of €9,300 purchased on credit from J. Brady entered in error in asset account and on incorrect side of Brady's Account as €9,500.

	Dr (€)	Cr (€)
Drawings Account	220	
Discount Allowed Account	30	
Debtor Account		250

Being private debt of €220 owed by Quinlan offset against a bill of €250 owed by a debtor.

	Dr (€)	Cr (€)
Wages Account	210	
Wages Accrued		210

Being the recording of wages due in books.

	Dr (€)	Cr (€)
Commission	900	
Creditor	950	
Capital		1,800
Discount Received		50

Being the recording of a private resource used to pay a business commission and a business debt.

	Dr (€)	Cr (€)
Creditors Account	1,770	
Suspense Account		1,770

Being a credit note received of €650 entered twice on incorrect side of creditor's account as €560.

Solution to Q 5.3(b)

Suspense Account

	(€)		(€)
J. Brady	19,000	Original Difference	17,230
		Creditors	1,770
	€19,000		€19,000

Solution to Q 5.3(c)

Statement of Corrected Net Profit

		(€)	(€)
Net Profit as per Accounts			24,000
Add			
Discount Received		50	50
			24,050
Less	Purchases	9,300	
	Discount Allowed	30	
	Wages	210	
	Commission	900	10,440
Corrected Net Profit			€13,610

Solution to Q 5.3(d)

Corrected Balance Sheet at 31/12/2001

	(€)	(€)	(€)
Fixed Assets			
Premises			120,000
Equip. (40,000 – 9,500)			30,500
			150,500
Current Assets			
Stock		140,000	
Debtors (15,000 + 17,230 – 250)		31,980	
		171,980	
Less Current Liabilities			
Creditors (80,000 + 18,800 – 950 – 1,770)	96,080		
Bank	30,000		
Wages due	210	126,290	45,690
			€196,190
Financed by			
Capital (194,000 + 1,800)		195,800	
Add Net Profit		13,610	
		209,410	
less Drawings (13,000 + 220)		13,220	
			€196,190

Question 5.4

The Trial Balance of P. O'Gorden, a grocer, failed to agree on 31 December 2000. The difference was entered in the Suspense Account. Trading and Profit & Loss Accounts and the following Balance Sheet were then prepared:

Balance Sheet at 31 December 2000

	(€)	(€)	(€)
Fixed Assets			
Premises			50,000
Delivery Vans at Net Book Value			20,000
			70,000
Current Assets			
Stock (including suspense)		22,000	
Debtors		8,000	
		30,000	
Less Current Liabilities			
Creditors	12,000		
Bank	2,000	14,000	16,000
			86,000
Financed by			
Capital		80,000	
Add Net Profit for the Year		9,000	
		89,000	
Less Drawings		3,000	86,000
			86,000

On checking the books, the following errors were discovered:

1. A motor van sold on credit for €4,600 to J. Collins was entered in both the sales book and on the incorrect side of J. Collins' Account as €6,400.
2. O'Gorden had returned goods €800 to a creditor and, prior to receiving the credit note, had entered this transaction in the books. However, the actual credit note, which later arrived from the creditor, showed a deduction of €20 for carriage. The only entry for this credit note had been €680 on the debit side of the creditor's account.
3. A cheque for €485 received from a debtor and a cash discount allowed of €15 had been entered correctly in the books. However, no entry had been made in the books of the subsequent dishonouring of the cheque or of the writing off of the account in full because of bankruptcy.
4. A credit note received from a creditor for €226 had been entered in the purchases returns book as €262 and posted to the credit side of the creditor's account as €202.
5. A debt of €400 owed to O'Gorden privately by a creditor was to be offset against the creditor's account in full settlement of an amount of €440 due to the creditor in the creditor's business account. No entry had been made in the books.

You are required to

(a) journalise the necessary corrections,
(b) show the Suspense Account,
(c) prepare a statement showing the correct net profit and
(d) prepare the corrected Balance Sheet.

Solution to Q 5.4(a)

P. O'Gorden

	Dr (€)	Cr (€)
Sales	6,400	
J. Collins	11,000	
Vans		4,600
Suspense		12,800

Disposal entered as Sale plus figure put on incorrect side.

	Dr (€)	Cr (€)
Purchases Returns	20	
Suspense	680	
Creditors		700

Reduction of €20 Credit Note dealt with incorrectly.

	Dr (€)	Cr (€)
Debtor	500	
Bank		485
Discount Allowed		15
Bad Debt	500	
Debtor		500

Dishonour of cheque plus write-off.

	Dr (€)	Cr (€)
Purchases Returns	36	
Creditors	428	
Suspense		464

Incorrect amounts entered.

	Dr (€)	Cr (€)
Creditor	440	
Capital		400
Discount Received		40

Business debt cleared by private debt.

Solution to Q 5.4(b)

Suspense Account

	(€)		(€)
Difference	12,584	J. Collins	12,800
Purchases Returns (Crs)	680	Creditors	464
	13,264		13,264

Solution to Q 5.4(c)

Adjusted Net Profit

	(€)	(€)	(€)
Net Profit Per Accounts			9,000
Sales	(6,400)		
Purchases Returns	(20)		
Discount Allowed		15	
Bad Debt	(500)		
Purchases Returns	(36)		
Discount Received		40	
	(6,956)	55	6,901
Corrected Net Profit			2,099

Solution to Q 5.4(d)

Corrected Balance Sheet at 31 December 2000

	(€)	(€)	(€)
Fixed Assets			
Premises		50,000	
Vans (20,000 – 4,600)		15,400	
		65,400	
Current Assets			
Stock (22,000 – 12,584)	9,416		
Debtors (8,000 + 11,000 + 500 – 500)	19,000		
	28,416		
Current Liabilities			
Creditors (12,000 + 700 – 428 – 440)	11,832		
Bank (2,000 + 485)	2,485		
	14,317		
Net Current Assets		14,099	
		79,499	
Financed by			
Capital (80,000 + 400)		80,400	
Add Net Profit		2,099	
		82,499	
Less Drawings		3,000	
		79,499	

Chapter 6

Tabular Statements

When answering questions regarding tabular statements, you should:

1. think through each figure before you write it down,
2. make sure each column agrees before you proceed to the next one and
3. remember that you are applying knowledge you have already learned in another area.

Question 6.1

The financial position of Macken Ltd on 1 January 2001 is shown in the following Balance Sheet.

Balance Sheet at 1 January 2001

	Cost (€)	Accumulated Depreciation (€)	Net (€)
Fixed Assets			
Land & Buildings	175,000		175,000
Motor Vehicles	69,000	29,000	40,000
	24,000	29,000	215,000
Current Assets			
Stock		56,000	
Debtors		39,000	
Insurance Prepaid		3,000	
		98,000	
Less Current Liabilities			
Creditors	46,000		
Bank Overdraft	24,000		
Expenses Due	1,500	71,500	26,500
			241,500

Continued

Balance Sheet at 1 January 2001 *Continued*

	Cost (€)	Accumulated Depreciation (€)	Net (€)
Financed by			
Share Capital			
Authorised: 250,000 Ordinary Shares @ €1 each			
Issued: 160,000 Ordinary Shares @ €1 each			160,000
Reserves			
Share Premium		40,000	
Profit & Loss		41,500	81,500
			241,500

January: Macken Ltd purchased an adjoining business which included buildings €85,000; Stock €34,000; Creditors €25,000. The purchase price was discharged by granting the seller 60,000 shares in Macken Ltd at a premium of 30 cent and €25,000 by cheque.

February: The remaining shares were issued at a premium of 30 cent.

March: Sold goods on credit for €72,000, which is cost price plus 20%.

April: Goods originally costing €500 were returned. Owing to their condition, a credit note for 20 per cent less than the selling price was issued.

May: €500 was received from a debtor previously written off as bad. This represented 25 per cent of the original amount, and the debtor has undertaken to pay the balance in September.

June: Paid a creditor a cheque for €600, having received a €30 discount.

September: Received balance of previously written-off debt as agreed in May.

October: Disposed of van for €9,000, which originally cost €17,000. The Book value of the disposed van was €8,000. Acquired new van for €20,000. Depreciation for the year on all vehicles was €11,000.

November: Purchased goods from supplier for a total cost price of €10,000. Paid half by cheque less 5 per cent discount. The other half was on credit.

You are required to record on a tabular statement the effects each of these transactions had on the relevant asset and liability and to ascertain the total assets and liabilities on 31 December 2001.

Solution to Q 6.1

Macken Ltd Tabular Statement

	(€)	Jan (€)	Feb (€)	Mar (€)	Apr (€)	May (€)	June (€)	Sept (€)	Oct (€)	Nov (€)	Total (€)
Assets											
Land & Buildings	175,000	85,000									260,000
Motor Vehicles	69,000								3,000		72,000
Depreciation	(29,000)								(2,000)		(31,000)
Stock	56,000	34,000		(60,000)	*480					10,000	40,480
Debtors	39,000			72,000	(480)	1,500		(1,500)			110,520
Insurance Prepaid	3,000										3,000
Goodwill		9,000									9,000
	313,000	128,000	0	12,000	0	1,500	0	(1,500)	1,000	10,000	464,000
Creditors	46,000	25,000					(630)			5,000	75,370
Bank	24,000	25,000	(39,000)			(500)	600	(1,500)	11,000	4,750	24,350
Expenses Due	1,500										1,500
Share Capital	160,000	60,000	30,000								250,000
Shared Return	40,000	18,000	9,000								67,000
Profit & Loss	41,500			12,000		2,000	30		(10,000)	250	45,780
	313,000	128,000	0	12,000	0	1,500	0	(1,500)	1,000	10,000	464,000

Working

***W1**

500 + 20% = €600
€600 – 20% = €480
Cost of Goods = €500
Value = €480
Use €480 as lower price — condition of goods.

Question 6.2

The financial position of CMW Ltd on 1 January 2001 is shown in the following Balance Sheet.

Balance Sheet at 1 January 2001

	Cost (€)	Depreciation (€)	Net (€)
Fixed Assets			
Land & Buildings	150,000		150,000
Vehicles	88,000	18,000	70,000
Goodwill	50,000		50,000
	288,000	18,000	270,000
Current Assets			
Stock		60,000	
Debtors		44,000	
		104,000	
Current Liabilities			
Creditors	37,000		
Bank	19,000		
Expenses Due	600	56,600	47,400
			317,400
Financed by			
Capital			
Authorised: 330,000 @ €1			
Issued: 220,000 @ €1			220,000
Reserves			
Share Premium		45,000	
Profit & Loss Balance		52,400	97,400
			317,400

The following transactions took place during 2001.

January:	Goods were sold on credit at a markup of 20 per cent for €6,000.
February:	CMW Ltd purchased an adjoining business made up of Buildings €65,000 and Stock €15,000. The purchase price was discharged by granting the seller 70,000 shares at a premium of 20 cent per share.
April:	Received cheque for €400 from a debtor and allowed a discount of €20.
June:	Delivery van originally costing €15,000 was traded against a new van costing €24,000. An allowance of €9,500 was made for the old van. Depreciation to date on the old van was €6,500, and the depreciation for the year was €15,000.
August:	Paid by cheque a creditor's account of €800 and received a 5% discount.
September:	Received first and final dividend of €80 from a debtor who was declared bankrupt. This amounted to 40 cent in the euro.
November:	Goods previously sold for €120 were returned. Because of the delay in returning the goods, a credit note for only €110 was issued.
December:	Received 50,000 from issue of remaining shares.

You are required to record on a tabular statement the effect each of these transactions had on the relevant asset and liability and to ascertain the total assets and liabilities on 31 December 2001.

Solution to Q 6.2

CMW Ltd Tabular Statement

	(€)	Jan (€)	Feb (€)	Apr (€)	June (€)	Aug (€)	Sept (€)	Nov (€)	Dec (€)	Total (€)
Assets										
Land & Buildings	150,000		65,000							215,000
Vehicles	88,000				9,000					97,000
Depreciation	(18,000)				(8,500)					(26,500)
Goodwill	50,000		4,000							54,000
Stock	60,000	(5,000)	15,000					100		70,100
Debtors	44,000	6,000		(420)			(200)	(110)		49,270
	374,000	1,000	84,000	(420)	500	0	(200)	(10)	0	458,870
Liabilities										
Bank	19,000			(400)	14,500	760	(80)		(50,000)	(16,220)
Creditors	37,000					(800)				36,200
Expenses Due	600									600
Share Capital	220,000		70,000						40,000	330,000
Share Premium	45,000		14,000						10,000	69,000
Profit & Loss	52,300	1,000		(20)	(14,000)	40	(120)	(10)		39,290
	374,000	1,000	84,000	(420)	500	0	200	(10)	0	458,870

Question 6.3

The financial position of Fuller Ltd on 1 January 2000 is shown in the following Balance Sheet.

Balance Sheet at 1 January 2000

	Cost (€)	Depreciation to Date (€)	Net (€)
Fixed Assets			
Land & Buildings	130,000		130,000
Furniture & Equipment	86,000	16,000	70,000
Goodwill	50,000		50,000
	266,000	16,000	250,000
Current Assets			
Stock		55,000	
Debtors		44,000	
Calls in Arrears		6,000	
		105,000	
Less Current Liabilities			
Creditors	41,000		
Bank	19,000		
Expenses Due	1,400	61,400	43,600
			293,600
Financed by			
Capital			
Authorised: 280,000 Ordinary Shares @ €1 each			
Issued: 200,000 Ordinary Shares @ €1 each			200,000
Reserves			
Share Premium		40,000	
Profit & Loss Balance		53,600	93,600
			293,600

The following transactions took place during 2000.

January: The shareholders who had failed to pay the 30 cent share at final call stage forfeited these shares, which were reissued at 80 cent per share fully paid.

February: Fuller Ltd purchased an adjoining business which included Buildings €70,000; debtors €16,000; creditors €20,000. The purchase price was discharged by granting the seller 60,000 shares in Fuller Ltd at a premium of 20 cent per share.

March: A payment of €300 was received from a debtor whose debt had been previously written off and who now wished to trade with Fuller Ltd again. This represents 20 per cent of the original debt, and the debtor had undertaken to pay the remainder of the debt by January 1994.

April: Goods previously sold for €150 were returned. The selling price of these goods

Continued on page 108

Solution to Q 6.3

Fuller Ltd Tabular Statement

	(€)	Jan (€)	Jan (€)	Feb (€)	Mar (€)	Apr (€)	May (€)	June (€)	Sept (€)	Nov (€)	Dec (€)	Total (€)
Fixed Assets												
Land & Buildings	130,000			+70,000								200,000
Furniture & Equipment	86,000										(800)	85,200
Depreciation	(16,000)										(350)	(15,650)
Goodwill	50,000			6,000								56,000
Current Assets												
Stock	55,000					+125						55,125
Debtors	44,000			+16,000	+1,200	(115)				(1,200)		59,885
Calls in Arrears	6,000	(6,000)										
Insurance Prepaid							+150					150
	335,000	(6,000)	0	+92,000	+1,200	+10	+150	0	0	(1,200)	0	440,710
Financed by												
Ordinary Shares	200,000	(20,000)	+20,000	+60,000					+20,000			280,000
Reserves												
Share Premium	40,000		+10,000	+12,000					+5,000			67,000
Profit & Loss Balance	53,600				+1,500	+10	+250	+40			+50	55,450
Forfeited Shares		+14,000	(14,000)									
Current Liabilities												
Creditors	41,000			+20,000				(760)			(500)	59,740
Bank	19,000		(16,000)		(300)		(300)	+720	(25,000)	(1,200)		(23,080)
Expenses Due	1,400											1,400
Rent Received Prepaid							+200					200
	355,000	(6,000)	0	+92,000	+1,200	+10	+150	0	0	(1,200)	0	410,710

was cost plus 20 per cent. Owing to the delay in returning these goods, a credit note for only €115 was issued.

May: Received a bank statement on 31 May showing a direct debit of €600 to cover fire insurance for year ended 31 March 2001 and a credit transfer received of €900 representing nine months' rent in advance from 1 June.

June: Settled by cheque a creditor's account of €760, receiving a discount of €40.

September: Received €25,000 from the issue of the remaining shares.

November: Received a balance of previously written-off debt as agreed in March.

December: A creditor who was owed €500 by Fuller Ltd accepted a computer, the book value of which was €450, in full settlement of the debt. The cost of this computer had been €800.

You are required to record on a tabular statement the effect each of these transactions had on the relevant asset and liability and to ascertain the total assets and liabilities on 31 December 2000.

Question 6.4

The following Balance Sheet shows the financial position of NYE Ltd at 1 January 2001.

Balance Sheet at 1 January 2001

	Cost (€)	Accumulated Depreciation (€)	Net (€)
Fixed Assets			
Buildings	180,000		180,000
Equipment	90,000	20,000	70,000
	270,000	20,000	250,000
Current Assets			
Stock		72,000	
Debtors		59,000	
Rates Prepaid		2,500	
		133,500	
Less Current Liabilities			
Creditors	45,000		
Bank	21,000		
Bills Payable	14,000	80,000	53,500
			303,500
Financed by			
Authorised Share Capital: 325,00 Ordinary Shares @ €1			
Issued: 175,000 @ €1			175,000
Reserves			
Share Premium		35,000	
Profit & Loss		93,500	128,500
			303,500

Continued on page 110

The following transactions took place during 2001.

January:	The company issued 50,000 shares at a premium of 25 cent.
February:	Paid by cheque a creditor's account of €1,200 and received a 5 per cent discount.
March:	Received a cheque for €800 from a debtor and allowed a discount of €40.
May:	Received €150 from a debtor who was declared bankrupt. This amounted to 30 cent in the €1. The remainder was written off.
June:	Purchased goods on credit. The recommended selling price was €4,200, which was cost plus 20 per cent.
August:	Purchased an adjoining business which included Premises €80,000; Vans €30,000; Stock €20,000; Creditors €25,000. The purchase price was discharged by the issue of the remaining shares at a premium of 25 cent per share.
September:	Received a credit note from a creditor for goods returned. These goods were purchased during June. Their retail price was €300, and a restocking charge of 10 per cent of cost was made.
November:	Sold goods on credit for €16,000. This represented cost plus $33\frac{1}{3}$ per cent.
December:	A creditor who was owed €750 by NYE Ltd accepted a computer in full settlement. The book value of the computer was €800 and had originally cost €1,100.

You are required to record on a tabular statement the effect each of these transactions had on the relevant asset and liability and to ascertain the total assets and liabilities on 31 December 2001.

Solution to Q 6.4

NYE Ltd Tabular Statement

	(€)	Jan (€)	Feb (€)	Mar (€)	May (€)	June (€)	Aug (€)	Sept (€)	Nov (€)	Dec (€)	Total (€)
Assets											
Buildings	180,000						80,000				260,000
Equipment	90,000									(1,100)	88,900
Depreciation	(20,000)									300	(19,700)
Stock	72,000					3,500	20,000	(250)	(12,000)		83,250
Debtors	59,000			(840)	(500)				16,000		73,660
Rates Prepaid	2,500										2,500
Bank	(21,000)	62,500	(1,140)	800	150						41,310
Vans							30,000				30,000
Goodwill							20,000				20,000
	362,000	62,500	(1,140)	(40)	(350)	3,500	150,000	(250)	4,000	(800)	579,920
Liabilities											
Creditors	45,000		(1,200)			3,500	25,000	(225)		(750)	71,325
Bills Payable	14,000										14,000
Share Capital	175,000	50,000					100,000				325,000
Share Premium	35,000	12,500					25,000				72,500
Profit & Loss	93,500		60	(40)	(350)			(25)	4,000	(50)	97,095
	362,000	62,500	(1,140)	(40)	(350)	3,500	150,000	(250)	4,000	(800)	579,920

Chapter 7

Depreciation and Revaluation

Questions on depreciation have always been popular with examiners and students. Questions on revaluation will also be easy to introduce into the examination. The key to success in both areas is to read through the questions carefully and to have a systematic approach.

1. It is vital that you show all your calculations as most of the marks are allocated for these.
2. With depreciation questions, determine immediately whether the depreciation is to be calculated from cost price or the written-down value.
3. Calculate carefully the total amount of depreciation written off from date of purchase to the beginning of the question for each fixed asset separately, showing all your figures.
4. With mid-year acquisitions/disposals, count off on your fingers slowly the number of months the asset was in the company's possession during the year in question.

To answer revaluation questions, consider the following:

1. This will involve Land & Buildings. Always remember that land is not depreciated. When land is revalued, this will simply mean an increase in the asset value.
2. When Buildings are revalued, the asset value is increased to the relevant amount and the accumulated depreciation is eliminated.
3. Further depreciation on the Buildings is usually calculated based on the remaining useful life of the Buildings.

Question 7.1
Mooney Transport Ltd prepares its final accounts to 31 December each year. The company's policy is to depreciate its vehicles at the rate of 20 per cent of book value per annum calculated from date of purchase to date of disposal and to accumulate this depreciation in the Provision for Depreciation Account.
On 1 January 2001 the company owned the following vehicles:

Vehicle No 1 purchased on 1 January 1997 for €35,000.

Vehicle No 2 purchased on 1 January 1998 for €40,000.

Vehicle No 3 purchased on 1 January 1999 for €44,000.

On 1 October 2001 vehicle No 1 was traded against a new vehicle costing €50,000. Vehicle No 1 had had a tachograph, which cost €6,000, fitted on 1 January 1999. The trade-in allowance was €15,000.

On 1 May 2002 vehicle No 2 was crashed and traded against a new vehicle costing €55,000. The company received compensation of €12,000 and the cheque paid for the new vehicle was €43,000.

Show, with workings, to the nearest euro for 2001 and 2002

(a) the Vehicles Account,
(b) the Provision for Depreciation Account and
(c) the Disposal Account.

Solution to Q 7.1 (a)

Vehicles Account

2001			(€)	2001		(€)
1 Jan	Balance B/D		125,000	1 Oct	Disposal	41,000
1 Oct	Trade-in	15,000				
	Bank	35,000	50,000	31 Dec	Balance C/D	134,000
			175,000			175,000
2002			**(€)**	**2002**		**(€)**
1 Jan	Balance B/D		134,000	1 May	Disposal	40,000
1 May	Trade-in	12,000				
	Bank	43,000	55,000	31 Dec	Balance C/D	149,000
			189,000			189,000

Solution to Q 7.1 (b)

Provision for Depreciation Account

2001		(€)	2001		(€)
1 Oct	Disposal	25,550	1 Jan	Balance B/D	58,184
31 Dec	Balance C/D	47,588	31 Dec	Profit & Loss	14,954
		73,138			73,138
2002		**(€)**	**2002**		**(€)**
1 May	Disposal	24,707	1 Jan	Balance B/D	47,588
31 Dec	Balance C/D	45,311	31 Dec	Profit & Loss	22,430
		70,018			70,018
			2003		
			1 Jan	Balance B/D	45,311

Solution to Q 7.1(c)

Disposal Account

2001		(€)	2001		(€)
1 Oct	Vehicle 1 + Tachograph	41,000	1 Oct	Depreciation	25,550
				Trade-in	15,000
				Profit & Loss	450
		41,000			41,000

2002		(€)	2002		(€)
1 May	Vehicle	40,000	1 May	Depreciation	24,706
	Profit & Loss	8,706		Trade-in	12,000
				Insurance Company	12,000
		48,706			48,706

Workings

W1

Vehicle 1

	Cost/Net (€)	Depreciation (€)	Net (€)
1997	35,000	7,000	28,000
1998	28,000	5,600	22,400
1999	22,400	4,480	17,920
2000	17,920	3,584	14,336
		(i) 20,664	
2001	(iii) 14,336 × 20% × 0.75	2,150	
		(ii) 22,814	

W2

Vehicle 2

	Cost/Net (€)	Depreciation (€)	Net (€)
1998	40,000	8,000	32,000
1999	32,000	6,400	25,600
2000	25,600	5,120	20,480
		(i) 19,520	
2001	(iii) 20,480	4,096	
2002	(iv) 16,384 × 20% × $\frac{1}{3}$	1,091	
	Total to disposal		24,707

W3

Vehicle 3

	Cost/Net (€)	Depreciation (€)	Net (€)
1999	44,000	8,800	35,200
2000	35,200	7,040	28,160
		(i) 15,840	
2001	(iii) 28,160	5,632	
2002	(iv) 22,528	4,506	

W4

Tachograph

	Cost/Net (€)	Depreciation (€)	Net (€)
1999	6,000	1,200	4,800
2000	4,800	960	
		(i) 2,160	
2001	(iii) 3840 × 20% × $\frac{3}{4}$	576	
		(ii) 2,736	

W5

Vehicle 4

	Cost/Net (€)	Depreciation (€)	Net (€)
2001	(iii) 50,000		2,500
2002	(iv) 47,500	9,500	

W6

Vehicle 5

	Cost/Net (€)	Depreciation (€)	Net (€)
2002	(iv) 55,000 × 20% × $\frac{2}{3}$	7,333	

(i) Depreciation to 2001	(ii) Depreciation Disposal 1	(iii) Depreciation 2001	(iv) Depreciation 2002
20,664	22,814	2,150	1,091
19,520	2,736	4,096	4,506
15,840		5,632	9,500
2,160	25,550	576	7,333
		2,500	
58,184		14,954	22,430

Question 7.2
High 'n' Mighty Plc purchased property on 1 January 1991 consisting of Land €150,000 and Buildings €340,000. The estimated useful life of the buildings was fifty years with a nil residual value at the end of the period. Depreciation is provided on a straight-line basis.

On 1 January 2001 the property was revalued to €960,000. Of this revaluation €300,000 was attributed to the land. (Land is not depreciated.) The remaining useful life of the buildings at the date of revaluation is to be left unchanged at forty years.

Show
(a) (i) Land & Buildings Account,
(ii) provision for Depreciation Account and
(iii) Revaluation Reserve Account all for 2001 and
(b) the relevant extracts from the final accounts relating to 2001.

Solution to Q 7.2(a) (i)

High 'n' Mighty Ltd
Land & Buildings Accounts

2001		(€)	2001		(€)
1 Jan	Balance B/D	490,000	31 Dec	Balance C/D	960,000
1 Jan	Revaluation Reserve	470,000			
		960,000			960,000
2002		(€)			
1 Jan	Balance B/D	960,000			

Solution to Q 7.2(a) (ii)

Provision for Depreciation Account

2001		(€)	2001		(€)
1 Jan	Revaluation Reserve	68,000	1 Jan	Balance C/D	68,000
31 Dec	Balance C/D	16,500	31 Dec	Profit & Loss	16,500
		84,500			84,500
			2002		(€)
			1 Jan	Balance C/D	16,500

Solution to Q 7.2(a) (iii)

Revaluation Reserve Account

2001		(€)	2001		(€)
31 Dec	Balance C/D	438,000	1 Jan	Land & Buildings	470,000
			1 Jan	Provision for Depreciation	68,000
		438,000			438,000
			2002		(€)
			1 Jan	Balance C/D	438,000

Solution to Q 7.2(b)

Balance Sheet at 31 December 2001

	(€)
Tangible Fixed Assets	
Land & Buildings	960,000
Less Depreciation	16,500
	943,000
Reserves	
Revaluation Reserve	438,000

Question 7.3

Moroney Ltd acquired property on 1 January 1992 consisting of Land €200,000 and Buildings €420,000. The estimated useful life of the buildings was forty years with a nil residual value at the end of the period. Depreciation is provided for on a straight-line basis.

On 1 January 2001 the property was revalued at €870,000. Of this, €350,000 was attributable to the land. Land is not depreciated. The remaining useful life of the buildings at the date of revaluation is to be left unchanged.

Show

(a) the Land & Buildings Account,
(b) the Revaluation Reserve Account and
(c) the Provision for Depreciation Account.

Solution to Q 7.3(a)

Moroney Ltd
Land & Buildings Account

2001		(€)	2001		(€)
1 Jan	Balance B/D	620,000	31 Dec	Balance C/D	870,000
1 Jan	Revaluation Reserve	250,000			
		870,000			870,000
2002		(€)			
1 Jan	Balance B/D	870,000			

Solution to Q 7.3(b)

Revaluation Reserve Account

2001		(€)	2001		(€)
31 Dec	Balance C/D	344,500	1 Jan	Provision for Depreciation	94,500
				Land & Buildings	250,000
		344,500			344,500
			2002		(€)
			1 Jan	Balance B/D	344,500

Solution to Q 7.3(c)

Provision for Depreciation Account

2001		(€)	2001		(€)
1 Jan	Revaluation Reserve	94,500	1 Jan	Balance B/D	94,500
31 Dec	Balance C/D	16,744	31 Dec	Profit & Loss	16,744
		111,274			111,274
			2002		(€)
			1 Jan	Balance B/D	16,744

Question 7.4

Midwest Transport Ltd prepares its final accounts to 31 December each year. The company's policy is to depreciate its vehicles at the rate of 20 per cent of book value per annum calculated from the date of purchase to the date of disposal and to accumulate this depreciation in the Provision for Depreciation Account.

On 1 January 2000 Midwest Transport Ltd owned the following vehicles:

Vehicle No 1 purchased on 1 January 1997 for €40,000.

Vehicle No 2 purchased on 1 January 1998 for €39,000.

Vehicle No 3 purchased on 1 January 1999 for €42,000.

On 1 September 2000 Vehicle No 1 was traded for €16,000 against a new vehicle costing €54,000. Vehicle No 1 had had a tachograph fitted on 1 January 1998 costing €6,000. On 1 April 2001 Vehicle No 3 was crashed and traded against a new vehicle costing €64,000. The company received compensation to the value of €8,000, and the cheque paid for the new vehicle which was €53,000.

You are required to show, with workings, to the nearest €1, for each of the two years 2000 and 2001,

(a) the Vehicles Account,
(b) the Provision for Depreciation Account and
(c) the Vehicles Disposal Account.

Solution to Q 7.4(a)

Midwest Transport Ltd
Vehicle Account

2000		(€)	2000		(€)
1 Jan	Balance	127,000	1 Sept	Disposal	46,000
1 Sept	Bank	54,000	31 Dec	Balance	135,000
		181,000			181,000
2001		**(€)**	**2001**		**(€)**
1 Jan	Balance	135,000	1 Apr	Disposal	42,000
1 Apr	Bank	64,000	31 Dec	Balance	157,000
		199,000			199,000

Solution to Q 7.4(b)

Provision for Depreciation Account

2000		Workings	(€)	2000		Workings	(€)
1 Sept	Disposal	W4	24,923	1 Jan	Balance	W1	44,120
31 Dec	Balance		37,752	31 Dec	Profit & Loss	W2	18,555
			62,675				62,675
2001		**Workings**	**(€)**	**2001**		**Workings**	**(€)**
1 Apr	Disposal	W5	16,464	1 Jan	Balance		37,752
31 Dec	Balance		46,306	31 Dec	Profit & Loss	W3	25,018
			62,770				62,770

Solution to Q 7.4(c)

Disposal Account

2000		(€)	2000		(€)
1 Sept	Vehicle No 1	46,000	1 Sept	Provision Account	24,923
				Allowance	16,000
			31 Dec	Profit & Loss	5,077
		€46,000			€46,000

Continued

Disposal Account *Continued*

2001		(€)	2001		(€)
1 Apr	Vehicle No 3	42,000	1 Apr	Provision Account	16,464
				Compensation	8,000
				Allowance	11,000
			31 Dec	Profit & Loss	6,536
		42,000			42,000

Workings

W1

Depreciation Balance 1 January 2000

Vehicle No	(€)	(€)
1	21,680	
2	14,040	
3	8,400	44,120

W2

Depreciation for 2000

Vehicle No	(€)	(€)
1	3,243	
2	4,992	
3	6,720	
4	3,600	18,555

W3

Depreciation for 2001

Vehicle No	(€)	(€)
2	3,994	
3	1,344	
4	10,080	
5	9,600	25,018

W4

Total Depreciation on Vehicle No 1

Depreciation	(€)	(€)
To 1 January 2000	21,680	
For 2000	3,243	24,923

W5

Total Depreciation on Vehicle No 3

Depreciation	(€)	(€)
To 1 January 2000	8,400	
For 2000	6,720	
For 2001	1,344	16,464

Question 7.5

On 1 January 1997 Quinn Ltd purchased buildings for €120,000. These buildings were expected to have a useful life of fifty years. During the year ended 31 December 1999, €38,000 was paid to a building contractor for an extension to the buildings. The company's own employees worked on the extension, and they were paid wages amounting to €10,000 by the company for this work. On 14 July 2000 the building was partially damaged by a storm, and the company spent €2,000 on repairs. On 1 January 2001 the building was valued by professional valuers at €230,000, and it was agreed to incorporate this revaluation into the company's accounts. It is the company's policy to apply a full year's depreciation in the year of acquisition.

The expected useful life of the extension was to be the same as the remaining useful life of the original building.

You are required to prepare the relevant ledger accounts in respect of the above transactions for the years ended 31 December 1997 to 31 December 2001.

Solution to Q 7.5

Buildings Account

Year		(€)	Year		(€)
1997			1997		
1 Jan	Bank	120,000	31 Dec	Balance C/D	120,000
1998			1998		
1 Jan	Balance B/D	120,000	31 Dec	Balance C/D	120,000
1999			1999		
1 Jan	Balance B/D	120,000	31 Dec	Balance C/D	168,000
	Bank	38,000			
	Wages	10,000			
		168,000			168,000
2000			2000		
1 Jan	Balance B/D	168,000	31 Dec	Balance C/D	168,000
2001			2001		
1 Jan	Balance B/D	168,000	31 Dec	Balance C/D	230,000
1 Jan	Revaluation Reserve	62,000			
		230,000			230,000

Buildings Accumulated Depreciation Account

Year		(€)	Year		(€)
1997			1997		
31 Dec	Balance C/D	2,400	31 Dec	Profit & Loss	2,400
1998			1998		
31 Dec	Balance C/D	4,800	1 Jan	Balance B/D	2,400
			31 Dec	Profit & Loss	2,400
		4,800			4,800
1999			1999		
31 Dec	Balance C/D	8,300	1 Jan	Balance B/D	4,800
			31 Dec	Profit & Loss	3,500
		8,300			8,300
2000			2000		
31 Dec	Balance C/D	11,800	1 Jan	Balance B/D	8,300
			31 Dec	Profit & Loss	3,500
		11,800			11,800
2001			2001		
1 Jan	Revaluation Reserve	11,800	1 Jan	Balance B/D	11,800
31 Dec	Balance C/D	5,000	31 Dec	Profit & Loss	5,000
		16,800			16,800

Building Repairs Account

2000		(€)	2000		(€)
1 Jan	Bank	2,000	31 Dec	Profit & Loss	2,000

Revaluation Reserve Account

2001		(€)	2001		(€)
31 Dec	Balance C/D	73,800	1 Jan	Buildings	62,000
			1 Jan	Building Accumulated Depreciation	11,800
		73,800			73,800

Chapter 8

Control Accounts

It is vital to know from where the figures in the Control Accounts come. The figures in the actual Control Account do not originate in the personal accounts; they are, in fact, taken from the nominal/general ledger accounts. In appearance the control is just the same as a personal account, and this causes confusion for some students. You must go back to basic book-keeping.

Let us go through the steps affecting Debtors. The approach is then the same for Creditors.

1. All credit sales are entered individually in the debtors' accounts and the total is entered in the sales accounts.
2. This is the same for returns, payments, discounts, etc.
3. At the end of the period, the accounts are balanced, and a list of all the debtors is drawn up.
4. At this stage only the Control Account is drawn up. This is done as a check/control on the accuracy of the list of debtors.
5. We go back to the accounts in the nominal ledger and take out the various total figures for the debtors' items. These are then entered in the Control Account, which is balanced.
6. The balance on the control account is then compared with the total of the list of debtors.

In these questions, differences have arisen, and we must, as in Suspense Accounts, reconcile the figures.

Question 8.1

On 31 December 2001 the Creditors Ledger Control Account of F. Short showed the following balances: €19,560 and €360. These did not agree with the list of balances because of the following.

1. An invoice received from K. Fahy for the purchase of goods at €900 less a trade discount of 30 per cent had been omitted from the books. (An item omitted will affect both the list of creditors and the control account, both of which should be increased.)
2. A credit note had been received from a supplier for €245. The only entry made in the books was €254 credited to the creditor's account. (This is missing from the Purchases Returns Account, and the figure in the Creditor's Account is both incorrect and on the wrong side.)
3. A discount of €85 was received and omitted from the books. (An omission means both sides must be reduced.)

4. A cash purchase of €300 had been credited to a supplier's account. (Cash purchases do not belong here at all.)
5. A creditor had charged Short €75 interest on an overdue account. The only entry made in the books had been €57 credited in the creditor's account. Following a complaint made by Short, this charge was reduced to €40 but had not been entered in the books. (In interest account, enter €40, and reduce creditor's account to €40.)
6. A credit note received from a supplier for €150 had been debited twice in the Purchases Returns Account but omitted from the creditor's account. (With purchases returns on the wrong side twice, a correction is then needed, and a reduction in creditor's account must be entered.)

You are required to show:

(a) the Adjusted Creditors Control Account,
(b) the Adjusted List of Creditors and
(c) a journal entry to correct error 5.

Solution to Q 8.1(a)

F. Short
Adjusted Creditors Control Account

	(€)		(€)
Balance	360	Balance	19,560
Credit Note (2)	245	K. Fahy (1)	630
Discount Received (3)	85	Interest (5)	40
Balance c/d	20,050	Credit Note (6)	150
		Balance	360
	20,740		20,740
Balance c/d	360	Balance B/D	20,050

Solution to 8.1(b)

Adjusted List of Creditors

	Plus (€)	Minus (€)	(€)
Original Balance			20,111
K. Fahy (1)	630		
Credit Note (2)		(499)	
Discount Received (3)		(85)	
Cash Purchases (4)		(300)	
Interest (5)		(17)	
Credit Note (6)		(150)	
	+630	(1,051)	(421)
Corrected Balance			19,690

Solution to 8.1(c)

Journal Entry

	Dr (€)	Cr (€)
Creditors	17	
Interest	40	
Suspense		57

Interest omitted from Interest Account and inverted figure in creditor's account.

Question 8.2

On 31 December 2000 the Creditors Ledger Control Account of P. Flynn showed the following balances: €26,940 and €140. These figures did not agree with the schedule (list) of creditors drawn up. An examination of the books revealed the following.

1. A credit note received for €340 had been entered in the books as €430.
2. Goods purchased on credit for €1,800 had been omitted from the books.
3. A discount received of €70 had been entered correctly. This had been subsequently disallowed, and the only entry made in the books had been €70 debited to the creditor's account.
4. A cash purchase of €300 had been credited to the creditor's account.
5. Bills Payable accepted of €900 had been entered twice in the creditor's account.
6. Flynn won a holiday voucher valued at €3,000. She gave half of this to a creditor as part-payment of her account. No entry had been made in the books.

You are required to show:

(a) the Adjusted Creditors Control Account and
(b) the Adjusted List of Creditors.

Solution to Q 8.2(a)

P. Flynn
Adjusted Creditors Control Account

	(€)		(€)
Balance	140	Balance	26,940
Holiday Voucher (6)	1,500	Credit Note (1)	90
Balance C/D	27,400	Purchases (2)	1,800
		Discount Received (3)	70
		Balance C/D	140
	29,040		29,040
Balance B/D	140	Balance B/D	27,400

Solution to Q 8.2(b)

Adjusted List of Creditors

	Plus (€)	Minus (€)	(€)
Original Balance			26,130
Credit Note (1)	90		
Purchases (2)	1,800		
Discount Received (3)	140		
Cash Purchases (4)		300	
Bills Payable (5)	900		
Holiday Voucher (6)		1,500	
	2,930	(1,800)	+1,130
Correct Balance			27,260

Question 8.3

On 31 December 2001 the Debtors Ledger Control Account of B. Cunningham showed balances of €25,560 and €80. These figures did not agree with the List of Debtors drawn up on the same date. An examination of the books revealed the following.

1. An invoice sent to a customer for €750 had been entered in the day books as €570.
2. Interest of €85 had been charged to a customer but had been entered as €95 in the customer's account. Following a complaint by the customer, this had been reduced to €40 but had not been entered in the books.
3. Cash Sales of €6,000 had been debited to a customer's account.
4. A discount of €30 was disallowed but had been treated as allowed in the customer's account.
5. Sales Returns of €400 had been omitted from the books.
6. A credit note for €150 was sent to a customer and entered in the books. The clerk forgot to deduct 10 per cent for a restocking charge and then sent and entered a second credit note for €135.

You are required to show:

(a) the Adjusted Debtors Ledger Control Account and
(b) the Adjusted Schedule of Debtors.

Solution to Q 8.3(a)

B. Cunningham
Adjusted Debtors Control Account

	(€)		(€)
Balance	25,560	Balance	80
Credit Note (6)	150		
Invoice (1)	180	Interest (2)	45
		Sales Returns (5)	400
		Balance C/D	25,365
	25,890		25,890
Balance B/D	25,365		

Solution to Q 8.3(b)

Adjusted List of Debtors

	Plus (€)	Minus (€)	(€)
Original Balance			31,430
Invoice (1)	180		
Interest (2)		(55)	
Cash Sales (3)		(6,000)	
Discount Disallowed (4)	60		
Sales Returns (5)		(400)	
Credit Note (6)	150		
	(390)	(6,455)	(6,065)
Correct Balance			25,365 (starting point)

Question 8.4
The Debtors Ledger Control Account of R. Gilmartin showed the following balances: €18,840 Debit and €390 Credit on 31 December 2001. These figures did not agree with the Schedule (List) of Debtors balances extracted on the same date. An examination of the books revealed the following.

1. Interest amounting to €64, charged to a customer's overdue account, had been entered as €46 in the Interest Account. Following a complaint by the customer, this charge was reduced to €36, but this reduction had not been entered in the books.
2. A discount to a customer of €15 was disallowed and had been treated as a discount allowed in the discount account.
3. Gilmartin had sent an invoice to a customer for €870. This had been entered in the appropriate day book as €780. However, when posting from this book to the ledger, no entry had been made in the personal account.
4. Bills Payable of €750 had been entered on the debit side of a debtor's account.

5. A credit note was sent to a customer for €105. The only entry made in the books was €15 debited to the debtor's account.
6. A customer's account had been credited with cash sales of €425.
7. A credit note for €160 was sent to a customer and entered in the books. However, the accounts clerk forgot to deduct a restocking charge of 10 per cent. When the error was realised, the clerk immediately sent another credit note for €144 and debited it to the debtor's account.

You are required to show

(a) the Adjusted Debtors Ledger Control Account and
(b) the Adjusted Schedule of Debtors showing the original balance.

Solution to Q 8.4(a)

Adjusted Debtors Ledger Control Account

	(€)		(€)
Balance	18,840	Balance	390
Discount disallowed (2)	30	Interest (1)	10
Invoice Error (3)	90	Credit Note Omitted (5)	105
Credit Note Error (7)	16	Balance	18,861
Balance	390		
	€19,366		€19,366
Balance b/d	18,861	Balance b/d	390

Solution to Q 8.4(b)

Adjusted Schedule of Debtors

	(€)	(€)
Balance as per list		18,202
Add Invoice Omitted (3)	870	
Cash Sales (6)	425	1,295
		19,497
Deduct Interest (1)	28	
Bills Payable (4)	750	
Credit Note Error (6)	120	
Restocking Error (7)	128	1,026
Balance as per adjusted Control Account		18,471

Question 8.5

On 31 December 2001 the Creditors Ledger Control Account of K. Cruise showed a credit balance of €19,955. This did not agree with the list of balances because of the following.

1. A discount disallowed of €80 had been omitted from the creditor's account but adjusted properly in the discount account.
2. Interest charged by a creditor of €95 had been entered only in the creditor's account and as €59.
3. Cruise returned goods of €320 to a supplier and entered this correctly in the books. However, a credit note arrived showing a deduction of 10 per cent for a re-stocking charge. The only entry for this was €280 debited to the creditor's account.
4. Bills Payable accepted of €1,100 had been omitted from the books.
5. Cruise received an invoice from a supplier for €675. This had been entered in the day book as €765.
6. Goods returned to P. Murphy of €450 had been entered in the books as €540.

You are required to show

(a) the Adjusted Creditors Control Account and
(b) the Adjusted Schedule of Creditors.

Solution to Q 8.5(a)

K. Cruise
Adjusted Creditors Control Account

	(€)		(€)
Bills Payable (4)	1,100	Balance	19,955
Purchases (5)	90	Interest (2)	95
Balance	18,982	Purchases Returns (3)	32
		P. Murphy (6)	90
	20,172		20,172
		Balance C/D	18,982

Solution to Q 8.5(b)

Adjusted List of Creditors

	Plus (€)	Minus (€)	(€)
Balance per Accounts			19,654
Discount Disallowed (1)	80		
Interest (2)	36		
Purchases Returns (3)	312		
Bills Payable (4)		(1,100)	
Purchases (5)		(90)	
P. Murphy (6)	90		
	518	(1,190)	(672)
Correct Balance			18,982

Chapter 9

Cash Flow Statements

Cash Flow Statements were introduced as a replacement for Funds Flow Statements under FRSI 1. They are mandatory for all companies except small private companies. They are in standard format which should be learned off. The format is as follows.

Operating Activities

Operating Profit
Plus Depreciation
Profit/Loss on Disposal
Increase/Decrease in Stock
Increase/Decrease in Debtors
Increase/Decrease in Creditors
Net Cash Inflow/Outflow from Operating Activities

Cash Flow Statement for Year Ended . . .

Operating Activities
Net Cash Inflow/Outflow from Operating Activities
Returns from Investment and Servicing of Finance
  Dividends Paid
  Dividends Received
  Interest Paid
  Interest Received
Net Cash Inflow/Outflow from Returns on Investment and Servicing of Finance
Taxation
  Taxation Paid
  Net Cash Outflow from Taxation
Investing Activities
  Acquisitions of Fixed Assets
  Disposals of Fixed Assets
  Net Cash Inflow/Outflow from Investing Activities
Net Cash Inflow/Outflow before Financing
Financing
  Issue of Share Capital
  Borrowing
  Repayment of Loans
Net Cash Inflow/Outflow from Financing
Increase/Decrease in Cash

When you know the layout of Cash Flow Statements, it makes your work easier. Take note also of the following.

1. If you are given the figures for Depreciation and Disposals, do not then also calculate them.
2. To find the amount of Dividends and Taxation paid, use T accounts.
3. Increase in Stocks is a minus. Then follow this through for Debtors and Creditors.
4. If you do need to calculate Disposals and Profit on Disposals, use T accounts.

Question 9.1
The following are the Abridged Profit & Loss Account and Balance Sheets of Dixon Plc.

Abridged Profit & Loss Account for the Year Ended 31 December 2001

		(€)	(€)
Operating Profit			650
Interest			60
			590
Taxation			230
Profit after Tax			360
Dividends	Interim	80	
	Proposed	70	150
			210

Balance Sheets

	31/12/01		31/12/00	
	(€)	(€)	(€)	(€)
Fixed Assets				
Land & Buildings	950		500	
Accumulated Depreciation	160	790	110	390
Machinery	360		430	
Accumulated Depreciation	150	210	140	290
		1,000		680
Financial Fixed Assets				
Investments		70		
Current Assets				
Stock	490		460	
Debtors	350		380	
Bank	40	880	60	900

Continued

Balance Sheets *Continued*

	31/12/01		31/12/00	
	(€)	(€)	(€)	(€)
Less Current Liabilities				
Creditors	430		400	
Taxation	230		180	
Dividends	70	(770)	60	(640)
Interest	40			
Working Capital		110		260
		1,800		940
Financed by				
Ordinary Shares @ €1		430		250
Reserves				
Share Premium		50		
Profit & Loss		300		90
Long-Term Liabilities				
12% Debentures		400		600
		1,180		940

You are also given the following.

1. Land & Buildings were acquired. There were no disposals.
2. Plant & Machinery were disposed of for €30,000.
3. Depreciation — Land & Buildings €50,000; Plant & Machinery €80,000.
4. Shares were issued for cash.

You are required to prepare the Cash Flow Statement for the Year Ended 31 December 2001.

Solution to Q 9.1

Dixon Plc
Net Cash Flow from Operating Activities

	Workings	(€)
Operating Profit		650
Depreciation		130
Profit on Disposal	W1	(30)
Increase in Stock		(30)
Decrease in Debtors		30
Increase in Creditors		30
Net Cash Inflow from Operating Activities		780

Cash Flow Statement for the Year Ended 31 December 2001

	Workings	(€)	(€)
Net Cash Inflow from Operating Activities			780
Returns on Investment & Servicing of Finance			
Interest Paid	W2	(20)	
Dividends Paid	W3	(140)	
Net Cash Outflow from Returns on Investment and Servicing of Finance			(160)
Taxation			
Taxation Paid		(180)	
Net Cash Outflow from Taxation			(180)
Investing Activities			
Purchase of Investments		(70)	
Sale of Plant & Machinery		30	
Purchase of Land & Buildings		(450)	
Net Cash Outflow from Investing Activities			(490)
Net Cash Outflow before Financing			(50)
Financing			
Issue of Shares at a Premium		230	
Repayment of Debentures		(200)	
Net Cash Inflow from Financing			30
Decrease in Cash			(20)

Proof

	2000 (€)	2001 (€)	Difference
Bank Balance	60	40	(20)

Provision for Depreciation Account

	(€)		(€)
Disposal	70	Balance	140
Balance	150	Profit & Loss	80

Workings

W1: Profit on Disposal

Machinery Account

	(€)		(€)
Balance	430	Disposal	70
		Balance	360

Disposal Account

	(€)		(€)
Machinery	70	Depreciation	70
Profit & Loss	30	Bank	30

W2: Interest Paid

Interest Account

	(€)		(€)
Bank Account	20	Profit & Loss	60
Balance	40		

W3: Dividends Paid

Dividends Account

	(€)		(€)
Bank Account	140	Balance	60
Balance	70	Profit & Loss (80 + 70)	150

Question 9.2

You work for a small limited company and are assisting in the preparation of the annual accounts for the year ended 30 November 2001. The following details are proved.

Brown Limited
Balance Sheet at 30 November

	2000			2001		
	(€)	(€)	(€)	(€)	(€)	(€)
Fixed Assets at Cost	259,500			365,100		
Less Depreciation	86,700		172,800	117,150		247,950
Current Assets						
Stock		111,600			108,120	
Debtors		146,880			150,030	
Bank		16,320				
		274,800			258,150	
Current Liabilities						
Creditors	62,160			55,620		
Overdraft				3,480		
Provision for Tax	25,680			18,600		
Proposed Dividend	15,000	102,840	171,960	18,000	95,700	162,450
			344,760			410,400
Financed by						
€1 Ordinary Shares			300,000			330,000
Reserves			44,760			80,400
			344,760			410,400

Brown Limited
Profit & Loss Account for the Year Ended 30 Nov. 2001

	(€)
Profit for the Year	72,240
Provision for Tax	18,600
	53,640
Undistributed Profits from Last Year	44,760
	98,400
Proposed Dividend	18,000
Undistributed Profits Carried to Next Year	80,400

Tasks: Prepare the Cash Flow Statement of Brown Limited for the year ended 30 November 2001.

Solution to Q 9.2

Brown Limited
Net Cash Inflow from Operating Activities

	(€)
Operating Profit	72,240
Depreciation for Year	30,450
Decrease in Stock	3,480
Increase in Debtors	(3,150)
Decrease in Creditors	(6,540)
Net Cash Inflow from Operating Activities	96,480

Cash Flow Statement for Year Ended 30 November 2001

	(€)	(€)
Net Cash Inflow from Operating Activities		96,480
Returns on Investment and Servicing of Finance		
Dividends Paid	(15,000)	
Net Cash Outflow from Returns on Investment and Servicing of Finance		(15,000)
Taxation		
Taxation Paid	(25,680)	
Net Cash Outflow from Taxation		(25,680)
Investing Activities		
Acquisition of Fixed Assets	(105,600)	
Net Cash Outflow from Investing Activities		(105,600)
Net Cash Outflow before Financing		(49,800)
Financing		
Issue of Shares	30,000	
Net Cash Inflow from Financing		30,000
Decrease in Cash		19,800

Proof

	2000 (€)	2001 (€)	Difference (€)
Cash at Bank	16,320		(16,320)
Bank Overdraft		(3,480)	(3,480)
Total			(19,800)

Question 9.3

You work for a small limited company and are assisting in the preparation of the annual accounts for the year ended 30 May 2002.

Aspen Limited
Balance Sheet at 30 May 2002

	2001			2002		
	(€)	(€)	(€)	(€)	(€)	(€)
Fixed Assets at Cost		173,000			243,400	
Less Depreciation		57,800	115,200		78,100	165,300
Current Assets						
Stock		74,400			72,080	
Debtors		97,920			100,020	
Bank		10,880				
		183,200			172,100	
Current Liabilities						
Creditors	41,440			37,080		
Overdraft				2,320		
Provision for Tax	17,120			12,400		
Proposed Dividend	10,000	68,560	114,640	12,000	63,800	108,300
			229,840			273,600
Financed by						
€1 Ordinary Shares			200,000			220,000
Reserves			29,840			53,600
			229,840			€273,600

Aspen Limited
Profit & Loss Account for the Year Ended 30 May 2002

	(€)
Profit for the Year	48,160
Provision for Tax	12,400
	35,760
Undistributed Profits from Last Year	29,840
	65,600
Proposed Dividend	12,000
Undistributed Profits Carried to Next Year	53,600

Tasks: Prepare the Cash Flow Statement of Aspen Limited for the year ended 30 May 2002.

Solution to Q 9.3

Aspen Ltd
Calculation of Net Cash Inflow/Outflow from Operations

	(€)
Operating Profit	48,160
Depreciation	20,300
Decrease in Stock	2,320
Increase in Debtors	(2,100)
Decrease in Creditors	(4,360)
Net Cash Inflow	64,320

Aspen Ltd
Cash Flow Statement for the Year Ended 30 May 2002

	(€)	(€)
Net Cash Inflow from Operating Activities		64,320
Returns on Investment and Servicing of Finance		
Dividends Paid	10,000	
Net Cash Outflow from Returns on Investment and Servicing of Finance		(10,000)
Taxation		
Taxation Paid	17,120	
Net Cash Outflow from Taxation		(17,120)
Investing Activities		
Acquisition of Fixed Assets	70,400	
Net Cash Outflow from Investing Activities		(70,400)
Net Cash Outflow before Financing		(33,200)
Financing		
Issue of Shares		20,000
Decrease in Cash		13,200

Proof

	2001 (€)	2002 (€)	Charge
Balance	10,880	—	10,880
Balance B/D	—	(2,320)	(2,320)

Question 9.4

Summarised balance sheets of Wantray Plc are as follows.

Balance Sheets

	31 July 2000		31 July 2001	
	(€'000)	(€'000)	(€'000)	(€'000)
Fixed Assets				
Cost	5,300		7,400	
Less Depreciation	1,650	3,650	2,290	5,110
Investments at Cost		300		100
Current Assets				
Stocks	2,100		2,400	
Debtors	1,600		1,450	
Cash	450	4,150	530	4,380
Current Liabilities				
Bank Overdraft	1,250		930	
Creditors	1,660		1,870	
Taxation	570		640	
Proposed Dividends	850	4,330	990	4,430
		3,770		5,160
Capital and Reserves				
Ordinary Shares of €1 Each Fully Paid		2,000		3,000
Share Premium Account				500
Profit & Loss Account		1,770		1,660
		3,770		5,160

During the year ended 31 July 2001, the following took place.

1. Fixed Assets which had cost €1,000,000 and on which depreciation of €300,000 had been provided were sold for €900,000.
2. Investments which had cost €200,000 were sold for cash at their book value.
3. 1,000,000 ordinary shares were issued for €1.50 per share.
4. Taxation due at 31 July 2000 was paid in full. Ignore advance corporation tax.
5. Dividends due at 31 July 2000 were paid. No interim dividends were paid.

Prepare the Cash Flow Statement for the year ended 31 July 2001 in accordance with FRS 1.

Solution to Q 9.4

Wantry Plc
Cash Flow Statement for the Year Ended 31 July 2001

	(€)	(€)
Net Cash Inflow from Operating Activities		2,320
Returns on Investments and Servicing of Finance		
Dividends Paid	(850)	
Net Cash Outflow From Returns On Investments And Servicing Of Finance		(850)
Taxation		
Corporation Tax Paid	(570)	
Tax Paid		(570)
Investing Activities		
Payments to Acquire Tangible Fixed Assets	(3,100)	
Receipts from Sale Of Tangible Fixed Assets	900	
Receipts from Sale of Investments	200	
Net Cash Outflow from Investing Activities		(2,000)
Net Cash Outflow before Financing		(1,100)
Financing		
Issue of Ordinary Share Capital	1,500	
Net Cash Inflow from Financing		1,500
Increase in Cash and cash equivalents		400

Reconciliation of Operating Profit To Net Cash Inflow from Operating Activities

	(€)
Operating Profit	1,520
Depreciation Charges	940
Profit on Sale of Tangible Fixed Assets	(200)
Increase in Stocks	(300)
Decrease in Debtors	150
Increase in Creditors	210
Net Cash Inflow from Operating Activities	2,320

Profit & Loss A/C to find operating profit

	(€)		(€)
Taxation	640	Balance	1,770
Dividends	990	Op. Profit	1,520
Balance	1,660		
	3,929		3,290

Chapter 10

Costing

1 Stock Valuation

'Stock should be valued at the lower of cost and net realisable value.' SSAP 9.

'Cost' is the expenditure incurred in bringing the stock to its location and condition.

'Net Realisable Value' is the estimated selling price less all further costs involved in getting it into saleable condition.

When materials are purchased at different prices during the year, a problem arises as to which price to use when valuing closing stocks. There are different methods, but FIFO is the only one which will be applied. This is also approved under SSAP 9.

2 Overheads and Absorption

The Overhead Absorption Rates to be used will be predetermined, based on machine hours, labour hours, etc.

$$\text{OAR} = \frac{\text{Total Overheads of Cost Centre}}{\text{Total Number of Absorption Units}}$$

Calculate the total overheads for the centre and then divide by the absorption units.

3 Apportionment

Where you have nonproduction departments, the overheads of these departments should be apportioned (allocated) among the various production departments. Build up the total overheads of all the departments in the first instance, and then proceed to eliminate the service departments among the other departments.

Service Department	Possible Basis of Apportionment
Canteen	Number of Employees
Maintenance	Value of Plant
Stores	Value of Materials
	Frequency of Requisitions

If you have, for example, two production departments, a maintenance department and a canteen, the two service departments will be eliminated. Start with the canteen and eliminate its overheads among the two production departments and the maintenance department. Only then eliminate the maintenance department.

Question 10.1

The New Irish Manufacturing Co Ltd has three separate workshops in one of its factories. The following data relate to this current year.

	Machine Shop	Assembly Shop	Finishing Shop
Direct Labour Hours	14,975	16,343	9,762
Hourly wage rates (€)	4.75	4.25	3.75
Variable Factory Overhead (€)	112,312.50	65,372	53,691

Total fixed factory overhead is expected to be €205,400.

A particular customer has requested a piece of specialist equipment, which will require materials from store of 1,000 kg at €4,173 per kilo together with components which will have to be purchased from outside suppliers amounting to €2,457. The packing and delivery costs will amount to €1,151. The following direct labour hours will be required to produce the equipment.

Shop	(hours)
Machine	140
Assembly	160
Finishing	100

Administration cost will be absorbed at 10 per cent of factory cost. For this type of job, it is the company practice to add 20 per cent of the selling price for profit.

You are required to prepare the detailed cost estimate and proposed selling price for this piece of specialist equipment.

Solution to Q 10.1

Specialist Equipment

	Rate	(€)	(€)
Direct Materials			
Materials ex Stores	1,000 kg @ €4.173		4,173
Bought-out Components			2,457
			6,630
Direct Labour			
Machine Shop	140 hr @ €4.75	665	
Assembly Shop	160 hr @ €4.25	680	
Finishing Shop	100 hr @ €3.75	375	1,720

Continued

Specialist Equipment *Continued*

	Rate	(€)	(€)
Variable Overhead			
Machine Shop	140 hr @ €7.50	1,050	
Assembly Shop	160 hr @ €4.00	640	
Finishing Shop	100 hr @ €5.50	550	2,240
Fixed Overhead	400 hr @ €5.00		2,000
Factory Cost			12,590
Administration 10% of €12,590			1,259
Packing and Delivery			1,151
Total Cost			15,000
Profit			3,750
Selling price			18,750

Calculations

	(€)	(€)
Variable Overhead Rates		
Machine Shop	$\frac{112{,}321.50}{14{,}975}$ =	7.50
Assembly shop	$\frac{65{,}372}{16{,}343}$ =	4.00
Finishing Shop	$\frac{53{,}691}{9{,}762}$ =	5.50
Fixed Overhead Rate	$\frac{205{,}400}{14{,}975 + 16{,}343 + 9{,}762}$ =	€5.00

Question 10.2

The Dai Ichi Co Plc has a budgeted capacity of 400,000 machine hours per annum. This capacity which, due to the recession, is only 80 per cent of the total capacity is used as the basis for accounting calculations. A typical budgeted quarterly production and sales, at a standard product mix, are 100,000 units.

The average selling price of the company's product range is €20 per unit and the contribution to sales ratio is 40 per cent. Three-quarters of the total variable costs are manufacturing, and the remainder apply entirely to selling and distribution. The budgeted fixed manufacturing costs are €0.75 per machine hour. The budgeted fixed selling and distribution costs are €500,000 per annum.

The company normally holds only minimal stocks, but as a result of the present economic climate, it is experiencing considerable fluctuations in sales and finds it has had to abandon this policy for the time being. In the recent second quarter, sales were 75,000 units at the standard product mix, whilst production was equivalent to 120,000 machine hours at the standard product mix. There were no stocks in existence at the start of the second quarter.

You are required to calculate the reported profit in the second quarter using variable costing and total absorption costing. Show by means of calculations exactly how the difference in the reported profits arise.

Solution to Q 10.2

Production per Annum (machine hours)			400,000
Sales per Annum (4 hrs × 100,000 units)		400,000	
		(€ per Unit)	(€ per Unit)
Selling Price			20
Variable Costs (60%)		12	
Manufacturing (75% of 60%)	9		
Selling and distribution (25% of 60%)	3		
Contribution (40%)		8	
Fixed Costs			
Manufacturing (1 machine hour @ 75 cent)	0.75		
Selling and Distribution (€500,000/400,000)	1.25	2	
Profit = Contribution – Fixed Costs			6

		Second Quarter	
		Variable (€)	Total Absorption (€)
Sales (75,000 @ €20)	1,500,000	1,500,000	
Cost of Sales (75,000 @ €12)	(900,000)		
Production (120,000 @ €9.75)		(1,170,000)	
Stock increase(45,000 @ €9.75)		438,750	
Gross Profit			768,750
Overabsorption (200,000 @ €0.75)		15,000	
Contribution	600,000		
Fixed Costs			
Manufacturing (100,000 @ €0.75)	(75,000)		
Selling and Distribution (€500,000/4)	(125,000)	(125,000)	
Variable Costs			
Selling and Distribution (75,000 @ €3)		(225,000)	
Profit		400,000	433,750

Difference: Stock movement × fixed manufacturing overhead per unit 45,000 × €0.75 = €33,750. This extra amount is included in the stock valuation in total absorption costing.

Question 10.3

You work in the cost office of Adams Ltd, a manufacturing company. There are three production departments and two service departments. Budgeted overheads for 2002 have been allotted to the department as follows:

	Production Departments			Service Departments	
	1	2	3	A	B
Overheads (€)	560,000	640,000	320,000	400,000	320,000

The service department cost for A and B are to be apportioned to production Departments 1, 2 and 3 as follows.

Department	1	2	3	A	B
A	40%	20%	20%		20%
B	50%	40%	10%		

Jobs are costed using the direct labour hour overhead absorption method and the budgeted direct labour hours for 2002 are

Department 1	92,000 hours
Department 2	110,000 hours
Department 3	88,000 hours

The budgeted direct labour wage rates for 2002 are

Department 1	€5.00 per hour
Department 2	€4.50 per hour
Department 3	€3.50 per hour

You are required to

(a) apportion the overhead costs of Departments A and B to the production departments,
(b) calculate the overhead absorption rates for the three production departments and
(c) if a product takes four hours in each production department and the basic raw materials used cost €80, calculate the total production cost.

Solution to Q 10.3(a)

Adams Ltd
Overhead Apportionment

Production Departments			Service Departments		
1€'000	2€'000	3€'000	A€'000	B€'000	Total €'000
560	640	320	400	320	2,240
160	80	80	(400)	80	
720	720	400		400	2,240
200	160	40		(400)	
920	880	440		0	2,240

Solution to Q 10.3(b)

OAR (Direct Labour)

$$\frac{920}{92} = €10$$

$$\frac{880}{110} = €8$$

$$\frac{440}{88} = €5$$

Solution to Q 10.3(c)

Product Cost

				(€)
Material				80
Labour	Department 1	€5 × 4	20	
	Department 2	€4.50 × 4	18	
	Department 3	€3.50 × 4	14	52
Overhead	Department 1	€10 × 4	40	
	Department 2	€8 × 4	32	
	Department 3	€5 × 4	20	92
				€224

Question 10.4

Roversby Ltd produce a specialised component for the catering industry. The company has two production departments — machinery and assembly — and a service department that maintains the heavy machinery and the air tools used in the assembly section. Budgeted costs for the coming year are as follows.

	(€)
Rent & Rates	40,000
Insurance of Machinery	25,000
Depreciation of Machinery	440,000
Supervisory Salaries	97,000
Maintenance Supervisor	20,000
Factory Cleaning	18,000
Rubbish Removal Contract	6,000
Lighting & Heating	150,000
Building Insurance	25,000
Indirect Materials	78,000
Maintenance of Fire Prevention Equipment	2,000

The following information is also available.

	Machinery	Assembly	Maintenance
Floor area (sq m)	4,000	2,500	150
Number of employees	50	120	6
Value of machinery (€)	900,000	120,000	

The factory works one seven-hour shift per day in the machinery department and one eight-hour shift per day in the assembly department (48 working weeks).

You are to

(a) prepare an analysis of the overheads showing the basis of allocation and apportionment to the three departments,
(b) re-allocate the maintenance overheads to the production departments,
(c) calculate an overhead absorption rate based on direct labour hours for each of the two departments,
(d) calculate the cost of a job which has the following costs:

	Machinery	Assembly
Direct Materials (€)	300	100
Direct labour (hr)	9	25
Wages rate (€)	5.50	5.90

(e) and briefly state what problems can arise when using the above method of allocation and apportionment.

Solution to Q 10.4(a)

Roversby Ltd
Overheads

	Percentage Apportioned	Machinery	Percentage Apportioned	Assembly	Percentage Apportioned	Maintenance	Total
Floor Area	60	4,000	37.5	2,500	2.5	150	6,650
Employees	28.5	50	68	120	3.5	6	176
Machinery	88	900,000	12	120,000			1,020

Solution to Q 10.4(b)

Roversby Ltd
Overhead Reallocation

	Machinery (€)	Assembly (€)	Maintenance (€)	Total (€)	Basis
Rent & Rates	24,000	15,000	1,000	40,000	FS
Insurance of Machinery	22,000	3,000		25,000	Value
Depreciation of Machinery	387,200	52,800		440,000	Value
Supervisory Salaries	58,200	36,375	2,425	97,000	FS
Maintenance Supervisor			20,000	20,000	
Factory Cleaning	10,800	6,750	450	18,000	FS
Rubbish Removal Contract	3,600	2,250	150	6,000	FS
Light & Heating	90,000	56,250	3,750	150,000	FS
Building Insurance	15,000	9,375	625	25,000	FS
Indirect Materials	46,800	29,250	1,950	78,000	FS
Maintenance of Fire Prevention Equipment	1,200	750	50	2,000	FS
	658,800	211,800	30,400	901,000	
	26,752	3,648	(30,400)		
	685,552	211,848			

Solution to Q 10.4(c)

Machinery
$7 \times 5 \times 48 = 1,680$ hrs; OAR = 685,552/1,680 = €408.07
Assembly
$8 \times 5 \times 48 = 1,920$ hrs; OAR = 211,848/1,920 = €110.34

Solution to Q 10.4(d)

Cost of Job

Direct Materials			
Machinery	300		
Assembly	200		400.00
Direct Labour			
Machinery	9 × 5.5	49.50	
Assembly	25 × 5.9	147.50	197.00
Overhead Maintenance	408.07 × 9	3,672.63	
Assembly	110.34 × 25	2,758.50	6,431.13
Budgeted Cost			7,028.13

Question 10.5

Ranelagh Ltd manufactures three products in two production departments, a machine shop and a fitting section; it also has two service departments, a canteen and a machine maintenance section. Shown below are next year's budgeted production data and manufacturing costs for the company.

Product		X	Y	Z
Production (units)		4,200	6,900	1,700
Prime Cost				
Direct Materials (€ per unit)		11	14	17
Direct Labour	Machine Shop (€ per unit)	6	4	2
	Fitting Section (€ per unit)	12	3	21
Machine Hours (per unit)		6	3	4

Budgeted Overheads

	Machine Shop (€)	Fitting Section (€)	Canteen (€)	Machine Maintenance Section (€)	Total (€)
Allocated Overheads	27,660	19,470	16,600	26,650	90,380
Rent, Rates & Light					17,000
Depreciation & Insurance of Equipment					25,000
Additional Data:					
Gross Book Value of Equipment	150,000	75,000	30,000	45,000	
Number of Employees	18	14	4	4	
Floor Space Occupied (sq m)	3,600	1,400	1,000	800	

It has been estimated that approximately 70 per cent of the Machine Maintenance Section's costs are incurred servicing the Machine Shop and the remainder incurred servicing the Fitting Section.

You are required to

(a) calculate the following overhead absorption rates: a machine hour rate for the Machine Shop and a rate expressed as a percentage of direct wages for the Fitting Section. All workings and assumptions should be clearly shown.
(b) Calculate the budgeted manufacturing cost per unit of each product.

Solution to Q 10.5(a)

Overhead Schedule

Expense	Basis of Apportionment	Machine Shop (€)	Fitting Section (€)	Canteen (€)	Machine Maintenance Section (€)	Total (€)
Allocated		27,660	19,470	16,600	26,650	90,380
Rent etc.	Area	9,000	3,500	2,500	2,000	17,000
Depr & Insurance	Book Value	12,500	6,250	2,500	3,750	25,000
		49,160	29,220	21,600	32,400	132,380
Apportionments						
Canteen	Number of Employees	10,800	8,400	(21,600)	2,400	
Maintenance	70:30	24,360	10,440		(34,800)	
		84,320	48,060			132,380

Calculation of Total Machine Hours

Product	X	Y	Z	Total
Machine Hours (per unit)	6	3	4	
Production (units)	4,200	6,900	1,700	
Total Machine Hours	25,200	20,700	6,800	52,700

Total overhead apportioned to the Machine Shop is €84,320. Therefore the Absorption Rate per Machine Hour is €1.60.

Calculation of Payroll total for Fitting Section

Product	X	Y	Z	Total
Wages (€ per unit)	12	3	21	
Production (units)	4,200	6,900	1,700	
Payroll Total (€)	50,400	20,700	35,600	106,800

Total overhead apportioned to the Fitting Section is €48,060. Therefore, the Absorption Rate as a percentage of Direct Wages is 48,050/106,800 × 100 = 45%.

Solution to Q 10.5(b)

Cost of Production (per unit)

	(€)	X (€)	(€)	Y (€)	(€)	Z (€)
Prime Cost						
Direct Materials		11		14		17
Direct Labour — Machine Shop		6		4		2
Direct Labour — Fitting Section		12		3		21
		29		21		40
Overhead						
Machine Shop (per machine hr)	9.6		4.80		6.40	
Fitting Section (per direct wages)	5.4		1.35		9.45	
		15		6.15		15.85
Cost of Production		44		27.15		55.85

Question 10.6

A picture-framing firm had the following transactions for the six months ended 31 December 2001. The figures are exclusive of VAT.

	Purchases		Sales
	2001	2001	
25 July	Purchased 150 units @ €20 each	15 Sept	Sold 305 units @ €45 each
28 Aug	Purchased 225 units @ €30 each	4 Oct	Sold 50 units @ €45 each
10 Nov	Purchased 410 units @ €40 each	23 Dec	Sold 100 units @ €75 each

Additional information.

1. The Balance Sheet at 1 July 2001 was as follows:

Bank Balance	€10,000
Capital Account	€10,000

2. Two months' credit is taken from suppliers.
3. One month's credit is given to debtors.
4. Expenses of €1,400 are paid each month as incurred.
5. Assume that purchases are liable to VAT at 10 per cent. Assume that sales are liable to VAT at 20 per cent.

You are required to

(a) calculate the value of closing stock at the end of each month during the period 1 July 1993 to 31 December 2001, using the first in, first out method (FIFO) and

(b) prepare the Trading and Profit & Loss Accounts and Balance Sheet for the six months ended 31 December 2001 and the Balance Sheet at that date.

Solution to Q 10.6(a)

Stock Valuation — FIFO

Date	Purchases			Sales			Balance	
2001	Units	€	Total	Units	Price	Total	Units	Total
25 July	150	20	3,000				150	3,000
28 Aug	225	30	6,750				375	9,750
15 Sept				305				

Continued

Stock Valuation — FIFO *Continued*

Date 2001	Purchases Units	Purchases €	Purchases Total	Sales Units	Sales Price	Sales Total	Balance Units	Balance Total
				150	20	3,000		
				155	30	4,650	70	2,100
4 Oct				50	30	1,500	20	600
10 Nov	410	40	16,400				430	17,000
23 Dec				100				
				20	30	600		
				80	40	3,200	330	13,200

Solution to 10.6(b)

Trading and Profit & Loss Accounts for 6 Months Ended 31 December 2001

	(€)	(€)
Sales		223,475
Less Costs Purchases	26,150	
Closing Stock	13,200	
Cost		12,950
Gross Profit		10,525
Less Expenses		8,400
Net Profit		€2,125

Balance Sheet at 31 December 2001

	(€)	(€)
Current Assets		
Stock	13,200	
Debtors (100 × 75 + 20%)	9,000	
Bank	7,825	
VAT Refund Due	140	
	30,165	
Less Current Liabilities		
Creditors (410 × 40 + 10%)	(18,040)	12,125
Financed by		
Capital	10,000	
Plus Net Profit	2,125	
		12,125

Chapter 11

Marginal Costing

'Marginal Costing' means finding the cost of producing $x + 1$ units instead of x units. It is also called 'variable costing' or 'contribution costing'.

It is not the cost of one unit or the cost of the first unit; rather it is the cost of producing 101 units instead of 100 units.

Costs are divided into two types: fixed and variable.

Fixed costs do not change with production and should be shown as one large figure. Variable costs alter with production and should be unitised.

Instead of Sales, we take Selling Price per unit.

$$\text{Selling Price} - \text{Variable Costs} = \text{Contribution (per unit)}$$

$$\text{Contribution} \times \text{Units Sold} = \text{Total Contribution}$$

$$\text{Total Contribution} - \text{Fixed Costs} = \text{Profit}$$

$$\frac{\text{Fixed Costs}}{\text{Contribution (per unit)}} = \text{Break even}$$

$$\frac{\text{Contribution}}{\text{Sales Price}} = \text{Contribution Sales Ratio}$$

Breakeven Charts

There are different acceptable methods by which breakeven charts may be drawn up. The one shown could be referred to as the 'traditional method'.

1. Draw the X and Y axes. The X, or horizontal, axis is for units, and the Y, or vertical, axis is for monetary values
2. Draw the Fixed Costs as a straight line parallel to the X axis.
3. Next draw the Total Costs line as a straight but sloping line, with the slope depending on the level of Variable Costs. (Note that you do not draw the Variable Costs as a separate line; rather they are the difference between Fixed and Total Costs.)
4. Then draw the Sales/Revenue Line as a straight/sloping line from the origin.
5. Where the Sales line intersects the Total Costs line is the Breakeven point.
6. The section above this represents Profit and the section below Loss.

Example

A company makes a product with a maximum capacity of €500,000 per annum. The unit selling price is €1, and the variable costs are €0.60 per unit. The fixed costs are €120,000. Draw a breakeven chart showing the profit at the projected sales/production level of 400,000.

$$\text{Selling Price} = 1.00$$
$$\text{Variable Costs} = 0.60$$
$$= \overline{\quad\quad}$$
$$\text{Contribution} = 0.40$$

$$\text{Break even} = \frac{120{,}000}{0.40}$$
$$= 3{,}000{,}000 \text{ units}$$

Question 11.1
The Irish Manufacturing Co Plc produces a single product. The cost per unit is as follows.

	(€)
Direct Material	12
Direct Wages (10 hours @ €5)	50
Overhead	68
Total	130

The fixed overheads amount to €800,000 and the above calculation has been obtained by dividing the total overheads incurred in the last period by the actual production of 20,000 units. These 20,000 units represent the normal capacity, but the factory can produce 25,000 units in the same period with no additional increase in fixed overheads. The company has an agreement with the union that the guaranteed minimum wage per period for direct workers will not be less than 180,000 hours at €5 per hour and overtime will be worked only when an excess of 20,000 units is produced and will be paid at time plus one-half. The company sells the units for €140.

You are required to

(a) calculate the Breakeven in units for the period and
(b) calculate the profit at 15,000, 20,000 and 25,000 units per period.

Solution to Q 11.1(a)
Separate the fixed and variable costs:

$$\text{Overhead} \times \text{units} = 68 \times 20{,}000 = 1{,}360{,}000$$
$$\text{Less Fixed Costs} = 800{,}000$$
$$\text{Total Variable Costs} = 560{,}000$$

$$\text{Unit Variable Cost} = \frac{560{,}000}{20{,}000} = €28$$

(Note: Regard Labour as fixed.)

Material = Unit Cost = 12
Overhead = 28
Total = 40
Selling Price = 140
Contribution = 100

Fixed Overheads = 800,000
Plus Labour = 900,000
Total = 1,700,000

$$\frac{1,700,000}{100} = 17,000$$

Solution to 11.1(b)

Profit Calculation

	Units					
Profit		@ 15,000		@ 20,000		@ 25,000
Total Contribution		1,500,000		2,000,000		2,500,000
Fixed Costs						
Overheads	800,000		800,000		800,000	
Labour	900,000		1,000,000		1,375,000	
Total		1,700,000		1,800,000		2,175,000
Profit/(Loss)		(200,000)		200,000		325,000

Question 11.2

You work as a product accountant for Gene's Jeans and are working on the planned estimates for the next year of one of your company's products.
The following are the budgeted costs of producing 12,000 units:

	€
Direct Labour	156,000
Direct Material	228,000
Production Overheads:	
Indirect Labour	24,000
Indirect Expenses	66,000
Administration Overheads	246,000
	720,000

You also have the following information.

1. The maximum possible capacity is for 14,000 units.
2. To obtain the selling price a markup of 25 per cent is used.
3. Your research into cost behaviour reveals that
   (i) indirect labour is 10 per cent variable,
   (ii) indirect expenses are estimated to be €3.60 per unit variable with the balance being fixed,
   (iii) direct labour and direct material are 100 per cent variable and
   (iv) all other costs are considered fixed.

You are required to

(a) prepare a suitable table to show fixed and variable costs based on an output of 12,000 units,
(b) calculate
   (i) the selling price,
   (ii) the contribution per unit and
   (iii) the breakeven point in units and
(c) prepare a breakeven chart based on 12,000 units of output, clearly indicating
   (i) area of loss,
   (ii) area of profit and
   (iii) margin of safety.
(d) If the price were reduced by 5 per cent output/sales would raise to 14,000 units. What would the profit be?

Solution to Q 11.2(a)

Gene's Jeans
Table of Costs

	Variable (€)	Fixed (€)	Total (€)
Direct Labour	156,000		156,000
Direct Material	228,000		228,000
Indirect Labour	2,400	21,600	24,000
Indirect Expenses	43,200	22,800	66,000
Administration Expenses		246,000	246,000
	429,600	290,400	720,000

Solution to Q 11.2(b)(i) Selling Price

$$\text{Total Costs} = 720{,}000$$

$$\text{Unit Costs} = \frac{720{,}000}{12{,}000} = €60$$

Selling Price = Cost + 25% = 60 + 15 = €75.

Solution to Q 11.2(b)(ii) Contribution per Unit

Contribution per Unit = Selling Price – Variable Costs

	(€)	(€)
Selling Price		75.00
Variable Costs		
Direct Labour	13.00	
Direct Material	19.00	
Indirect Labour	0.20	
Indirect Expenses	3.60	35.80
Contribution		39.20

Solution to Q 11.2(b)(iii) Breakeven Point

$$\text{Breakeven} = \frac{\text{Fixed Costs}}{\text{Contribution per unit}}$$

$$= \frac{290{,}400}{39.20} = 7{,}408 \text{ units}$$

Solution to Q 11.2(c)

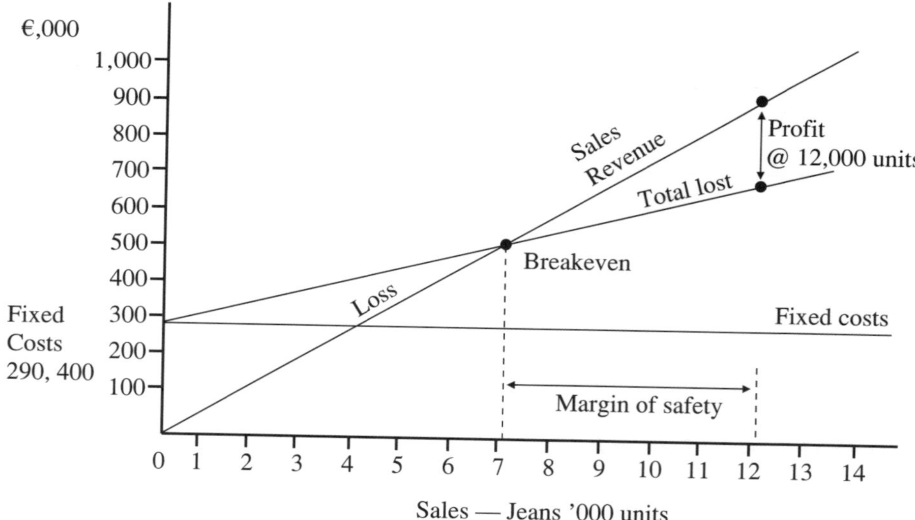

Solution to Q 11.2(d)

$$\text{Selling Price} - 5\% = \text{Units Sold}$$
$$\text{Selling Price} = 75 - 5\% = 71.25$$

$$\begin{array}{lcr} \text{Less Variable Costs} & & 35.80 \\ & = & \overline{} \\ \text{Contribution} & & 35.45 \end{array}$$

$$\text{Total Contribution} = 35.45 \times 14{,}000 = 496{,}300$$
$$\text{Profit} = \text{Total Contribution} - \text{Fixed Costs}$$
$$205{,}900 = 496{,}300 - 290{,}400$$

$$\text{Profit @ } 12{,}000 \text{ units} = (39.20 \times 12{,}000) - 290{,}400 = 180{,}000$$

Question 11.3

The Supreme Irish Manufacturing Co Plc at the moment operates at 70 per cent capacity owing to the current state of the economy. In recent years it has concentrated on manufacturing one particular product only, a small AC electric motor. The costs of production for the four weeks ended 27 August 2001 were

	€
Direct Materials	68,040
Direct Wages	10,206
Overhead	27,385

Sales of 1,701 AC electric motors amounted to €110,565 during this period in which there were no stock movements of raw materials, work-in-progress or finished goods.

Recently a Chinese importer has asked you to quote for the supply of 750 of these motors on a one-off basis to be supplied before 1 November 2001. Delivery will take five weeks and will cost €7,250, and production will commence on 29 August 2001 and delivery will start on 25 September 2001. These motors will be incorporated into another product and will not influence the current market price in any way.

The management is anxious to secure a footing in the Chinese market, is willing to quote an exact breakeven price in the circumstances and has ascertained that overhead at 100 per cent capacity will amount to €32,488 and that variable overheads are linear with production. At present no finished stocks of motors exist.

You are required to calculate the breakeven price in these circumstances for the 750 motors in total assuming 1,701 motors would also be sold in the four weeks to 25 September 2001 if the Chinese order were not accepted.

Solution to Q 11.3

Production commences 29 August 2001, and delivery commences 25 September 2001. This allows four weeks for production. Five weeks has been allowed for delivery.

$$\frac{1{,}701}{0.7} = 2{,}340 = 100\% \text{ capacity}$$

Overhead

Capacity (%)	(€)	Units
100	32,488	2,430
70	27,385	1,701
	5,103	729

Variable Overhead per Motor, $\frac{€5{,}103}{729} = €7$

Fixed Overhead, €15,478 = €27,385 – (1,701 × €7)

Direct Material per Motor, $\frac{€68{,}040}{1{,}701} = €40$

Direct Wages per Motor $\frac{€10{,}206}{1{,}701} = €6$

Selling Price per Motor $\frac{€110{,}565}{1{,}701} = €65$

Breakeven Price for 750 Motors

		(€)
Direct Materials	750 × €40	30,000
Direct Wages	750 × €6	4,500
Variable Overheads	750 × €7	5,250
Lost Contribution	21 × €12	252
Delivery	21 × €12	252
		7,250
		47,252

If the 750 motors are produced and sold, 21 i.e. (750 – 729) will not be available for normal sales so contribution of €12, i.e. €65 – (40 + 6 + 7) will be lost on these sales.

Question 1.4

You work as a Project Accountant for Work To Rule Ltd manufacturing company and are preparing costings for one of the company's products.

The following is the cost per unit based on a production level of 10,000 units. (Note: The company has the capacity to make 14,000 units.)

	€
Direct Material	30
Direct Labour	20
Factory Overheads	
Variable	8
Fixed	10
Administrative Overheads — Fixed	4
Selling & Distribution Overheads (60% Fixed)	10
	82
Current Selling Price	120

The following proposals have to be evaluated.

(i) Reduce the price by 10 per cent, which would increase the number sold by 20 per cent.
(ii) Pay a sales commission of €5 per unit, which would increase the number sold by 15 per cent.
(iii) Make a design change that will increase the variable cost by €8 per unit, which would increase the number sold by 20 per cent.

You are required to

(a) compute the existing Contribution per Unit,
(b) compute the existing total Fixed Costs,
(c) compute the profit under Proposal (i) above,
(d) compute the profit under Proposal (ii) and
(e) compute the profit under Proposal (iii).

Solution to Q 11.4(a)

Contribution per Unit

	(€)	(€)
Selling Price		120
Variable Costs		
Direct Material	30	
Direct Labour	20	
Overheads	8	
Selling & Distribution	4	62
Contribution		58

Solution to Q 11.4(b)

Fixed Costs

Factory Overheads	10 × 10,000	100,000
Administration	4 × 10,000	40,000
Selling & Distribution	(10 × 60%) × 10,000	60,000
		200,000

Existing Contribution = 58 × 10,000 = 580,000
Less Fixed Costs = 200,000
Profit = 380,000

Solution to Q 11.4(c)

To compute the profit for proposal (i):

Selling Price = 120 – 10% = 108
Variable Costs = 58
Contribution = 50
Total Contribution = 50 × 12,000 = 600,000
Less Fixed Costs = 200,000
Profit = 400,000

Solution to Q 11.4(d)

To compute the profit for Proposal (ii)

Selling Price = 120
Variable Costs = 62 + 5 = 67
(i.e. 58 – 5) Contribution = 53

Total Contribution = 53 × 11,500 = 609,500
Less Fixed Costs = 200,000
Profit = €409,500

Solution to Q 11.4(e)

To compute the profit for Proposal (iii)

Selling Price = 120
Variable Costs = 62 + 8 = 70
Contribution = 50

Total Contribution = 50 × 12,000 = 600,000
Less Fixed Costs = 200,000
Profit = 400,000

Question 11.5

The account of Astor Plc is currently evaluating three proposals put forward for discussion by the sales marketing team.

Current Position for 50,000 Units

	(€000s)	(€000s)
Sales (50,000 units)		2,500
Direct Materials	750	
Direct Labour	525	
Fixed Overheads	900	2,175
Profit		325

Proposal (i): To reduce the selling price by €5 per unit and increase advertising costs by €30,000. It is anticipated that this should increase sales volume by 15 per cent.

Proposal (ii): To use a better-quality material in the manufacturing process. This will increase the material costs by €3 per unit, but as it is easier to work with, there will be less reworking to be done, saving €1 per unit in labour costs. Additional advertising will be necessary to promote the 'new image' product. This will cost €60,000 and should result in an increase in sales of 5,000 units.

Proposal (iii): Install new computerised equipment which will cut labour costs by 50 per cent. This proposal will necessitate using better quality material at an additional cost of €3 per unit. As a special introductory offer for the new product, the company would pass on 40 per cent of the labour cost's savings to the customers. Sales are expected to increase to 65,000 units with additional costs of €25,250.

You are to evaluate each proposal and recommend, with reasons, which one (if any) management should adopt.

Solution to Q 11.5

Contribution per Unit

			(€)
Selling Price		50.00	
Variable Costs			
Direct Materials	15.00		
Direct Labour	10.50	25.50	
Contribution		24.50	
Total Contribution (24.50 × 50,000)			1,225,000
Less Fixed Costs			900,000
Profit			325,000

Proposal (i)

	(€)
Selling Price	45.00
Less Variable Costs	25.50
Contribution	19.50
Total Contribution (19.50 × 57,500)	1,121,250
Less Fixed Costs	930,000
Profit	191,250

Proposal (ii)

	(€)	(€)	
Selling Price		50.00	
Direct Materials	18.00		
Direct Labour	9.50		
		27.50	
Contribution		22.50	
Total Contribution (22.50 × 55,000)			1,237,500
Less Fixed Costs			960,000
Profit			€277,500

Proposal (iii)

	(€)	(€)
Selling Price	50 – 2.10	47.90
Less Variable Costs		
Direct Materials	18.00	
Direct Labour	5.25	23.45
Contribution		24.65
Total Contribution (65,000 × 24.65)		1,602,250
Less Fixed Costs		925,250
Profit		677,000

Proposal (iii) should be adopted as this easily gives the highest profit. Proposals (i) and (ii) yield lower profits than the present position.

All of these computations assume that the figures are accurate and that agreement can be obtained for each proposal. If Proposal (iii) leads to redundancy, a once-off figure for redundancy payment will have to be included.

Question 11.6

You work for the project account in a company which is about to launch a new product onto the market. Substantial market research and cost accounting activity have already taken place, and you have a number of scenarios for which to prepare contribution analyses.

Initial Budgeted Data

Sales in Units*	50,000
Variable Cost (per unit €)	
Direct Material	40
Direct Wages	50
Overheads	30
	120

* Maximum capacity available = 70,000 units.

Selling price is €160. Fixed overheads attributed to the product total €800,000.

Scenario (i): Decrease the price to €154, which would increase sales to 63,000 units.

Scenario (ii): Spend another €20,000 on promotional activity, which would increase sales to 65,000 units.

Scenario (iii): Increase the price to €165 and spend another €300,000 on promotional activity which would increase sales to 54,000 units.

You are to

(a) compute the existing budgeted profit,
(b) compute the profit under Scenario (i),
(c) compute the profit under Scenario (ii) and
(d) compute the profit under Scenario (iii).
(e) Comment on the four possible scenarios, and state which one you would choose.

Solution to Q 11.6(a)

Product Launch
Existing Budgeted Profit

	(€)	(€)
Selling Price		160
Less Variable Costs		
Direct Materials	40	
Direct Wages	50	
Variable Overheads	30	120
Contribution		40
Total Contribution (40 × 50,000)		2,000,000
Less Fixed Costs		800,000
Profit		1,200,000

Solution to Q 11.6(b)

	(€)	(€)
Selling Price	154	
Less Variable Costs	120	
Contribution	34	(or 40 – 6)
Total Contribution (34 × 63,000)		2,142,000
Less Fixed Costs		800,000
Profit		1,342,000

Solution to Q 11.6(c)

	(€)	(€)
Contribution	40	
Total Contribution (€40 × 65,000)		2,600,000
Less Fixed Costs		820,000
Profit		1,780,000

Solution to 11.6(d)

	(€)	
Selling Price	165,000	
Less Variable Costs	120	
Contribution	45	(or 40 + 5)
Total Contribution (45 × 54,000)	2,430,000	
Less Fixed Costs	1,100,000	
Profit	1,330,000	

Solution to 11.6(e)

All four proposals are profitable but (c) i.e. scenario (ii) yields the highest profit and with only a marginal expenditure of €20,000.

Chapter 12

Budgets

Subsidiary Budgets

Sales Budget = Budgeted Unit Sales × Budgeted Selling Price
Production Budget = Budgeted Sales + Budgeted Closing Stock – Budgeted Opening Stock
Materials Usage Budget = Production Units × Units of Different Materials Required per Product
Materials Purchase Budget = Materials Usage Budget + Closing Stock of Materials – Opening Stock of Materials

Principal Budgets

There are 3 principal budgets.

1. Cash Budget
2. Budgeted Profit & Loss Account
3. Budgeted Balance Sheet.

Great care needs to be taken in drawing up these budgets. An examination, done a year later, of business start-up plans submitted to financial institutions revealed that over 90 per cent were seriously in error. Sales and the ability to collect had been seriously overestimated. Cost of Sales and the ability to obtain credit had been seriously under- and overestimated. The amount of various expenses had been underestimated. This has been identified as a major cause of new business failure.

1. Cash Budgets for Examination Purposes.

(a) Remember only actual receipts and payments are included.
(b) These are included when actually received and paid not when due.
(c) Depreciation is always excluded (non-cash item).
(d) Credit Sales and Purchases at end of period are excluded.
(e) Changes in stock levels will affect Cash Budgets.
(f) The closing balance at end of period one is equal to the opening balance at beginning of period two.

2. Budgeted Profit & Loss Account

(a) If you are using a Total column in your Cash Budget, the Total figure does not necessarily become the Profit & Loss figure.
(b) Include all Sales/Purchases, i.e. both Cash and Credit for the period.
(c) Exclude accruals at the beginning and prepayments at the end of the period.
(d) Include Depreciation.

(**Note:** Many budgets are for six months, and the depreciation will be per annum. So remember to allocate properly.)

(e) Exclude capital expenditure.

3. Budgeted Balance Sheet

(a) Include the total of all fixed assets and the relevant depreciation.
(b) Ensure that you calculate the closing stock figure at the cost price not the selling price.
(c) Debtors = Unpaid Credit Sales.
(d) The Cash figure is closing cash figure from your Cash Budget.
(e) Creditors = Unpaid Credit Purchases.
(f) Include accruals and prepayments at the period end.

Question 12.1

The East Roscommon Manufacturing Company Plc manufactures three products: A, B and C.

Sales Data for the Month of February

Product	Quantity	Unit Price (€)
A	1,000	100
B	2,000	120
C	1,500	140

The materials used in the company's products are as follows.

Material	M1	M2	M3
Unit Cost (€)	4	6	9

The quantities used are as follows.

Product:	M1 (units)	M2 (units)	M3 (units)
A	4	2	
B	3	3	2
C	2	1	1

The finished stocks are as follows.

	Product		
	A (units)	B (units)	C (units)
1 February	1,000	1,500	500
28 February	1,100	1,650	550

The materials stocks are as follows.

	Material		
	M1 (units)	M2 (units)	M3 (units)
1 February	26,000	20,000	12,000
28 February	31,200	24,000	14,400

You are required to prepare for the month of February,

(a) the Sales Budget,
(b) the Production Budget,
(c) the Materials Usage Budget and
(d) the Materials Purchase Budget.

Solution to Q 12.1(a)

East Roscommon Manufacturing Company Plc
Sales Budget

	Products			
	A	B	C	
Sales Quantities (units)	1,000	2,000	1,500	
Selling Price (€)	100	120	140	
Sales Value (€)	100,000	240,000	210,000	
Total (€)				550,000

Solution to Q 12.1(b)

Production Budget

	Products		
	A (units)	B (units)	C (units)
Sales	1,000	2,000	1,500
Closing stock	1,100	1,650	550
	2,100	3,650	2,050
Less Opening Stock	1,000	1,500	500
Required Production	1,100	2,150	1,550

Solution to Q 12.1(c)

Material Usage Budget

		Materials					
		M1		M2		M3	
	Production	Units	Total	Units	Total	Units	Total
A	1,100	4	4,400	2	2,200		
B	2,150	3	6,450	3	6,450	2	4,300
C	1,550	2	3,100	1	1,550	1	1,550
Total Units			13,950		10,200		5,850

Solution to Q 12.1(d)

Materials Purchase Budget

	Materials			
	M1	M2	M3	
Usage (units)	13,950	10,200	5,850	
Add Closing Stock (units)	31,200	24,000	14,400	
	45,150	34,200	20,250	
Less Opening Stock (units)	26,000	20,000	12,000	
Required Purchases (units)	19,150	14,200	8,250	
Unit Cost (€)	4	6	9	
Value (€)	76,600	85,200	74,250	
Total (€)				236,050

Question 12.2

The Just-In-Time Production Co had the following Sales Budget for the first five months of the year.

Sales Budget

	Jan	Feb	Mar	Apr	May
Units	8,000	10,000	14,000	18,000	20,000

The stock control policy requires that month-end stocks should comprise Raw Materials representing 25 per cent of next month's production requirements and finished goods representing 20 per cent of next month's sales.

Stock at 1 January

	(units)
Raw Materials	5,000
Finished Goods	1,600

Each unit of Finished Goods requires two units of Raw Material.

The production process is such that there is no Work-in-Progress at the end of the day.
You are required to

(a) prepare a Production Budget for each of the first three months of the year and
(b) show what the stock of Raw Materials will be at the end of each of the first three months of the year.

Solution to Q 12.2(a)

Just-In-Time Production Co
Production Budget

	Jan (units)	Feb (units)	Mar (units)
Sales	8,000	10,000	14,000
Closing Stock	2,000	2,800	3,600
	10,000	12,800	17,600
Opening Stock	1,600	2,000	2,800
Units to Be Produced	8,400	10,800	14,800

Solution to Q 12.2(b)

Raw Materials Stock at End of Each Month = Next Month's Production × 25% × 2

i.e. two units of Raw Material for each unit of Finished Goods.

January = 10,800 × 2 × 25% = 5,400
February = 14,800 × 2 × 25% = 7,400
March = Production April (18,000 + 4,000 – 3,600) = 18,400 × 2 × 25% = 9,200

Question 12.3

A friend of yours, C. Priestly, is thinking of setting up in business and has drawn up the following plans.

1. On 1 September 2002 Priestly plans to deposit €120,000 in a business bank account.
2. On 2 September 2002 Priestly plans to buy and pay for premises with €70,000.
3. On 3 September 2002 he plans to buy other fixed assets for €50,000, half of which is to be paid in September and the other half in December.
4. He plans to employ two sales assistants whose monthly wages amount to €1,300, payable at the end of each month (ignore Tax & Insurance).
5. He plans to sell the following goods.

	Sept	Oct	Nov	Dec	Jan	Feb
Units	450	550	600	600	750	800

   Units will be sold on a credit basis for €50 each, and debtors are expected to settle their accounts two months after the month in which goods are sold.
6. He plans to buy the following goods.

	Sept	Oct	Nov	Dec	Jan	Feb
Units	1,000	500	500	600	700	800

   Units will cost €20 each, and suppliers expect to be paid in the month following the month in which the goods are bought.
7. Other expenses are estimated at €850 per month payable one month in arrears.
8. Priestly expects to make monthly cash drawings of €1,500.
9. All assets, other than premises, are to be depreciated at the rate of 10 per cent per annum. Premises are to be depreciated at the rate of 5 per cent per annum.

You are required to

(a) prepare the Schedule of Payments for the six months ending February 2003,
(b) prepare the Cash Budget for the six months ending February 2003 and

(c) prepare the Budgeted Trading and Profit & Loss Accounts and Balance Sheet for the period ending 28 February 2003.

Solution to Q 12.3(a)

Sales Budget

	Sept	Oct	Nov	Dec	Jan	Feb
Units	450	550	600	600	750	800
Total (€)	22,500	27,500	30,000	30,000	37,500	40,000
Receipts (€)			22,500	27,500	30,000	30,000

Purchases Budget

	Sept	Oct	Nov	Dec	Jan	Feb
Units	1,000	500	500	600	700	800
Total (€)	20,000	10,000	10,000	12,000	14,000	16,000
		20,000	10,000	12,000	12,000	14,000

Solution to Q 12.3(b)

Cash Budget

	Sept	Oct	Nov	Dec	Jan	Feb	Total
Inflows							
Sales (€)			22,500	27,500	30,000	30,000	110,000
Outflows							
Purchases (€)		20,000	10,000	10,000	12,000	14,000	66,000
Premises (€)	70,000						70,000
Fixed Assets (€)	25,000			25,000			50,000
Wages (€)	1,300	1,300	1,300	1,300	1,300	1,300	7,800
General Expenses (€)		850	850	850	850	850	4,250
Drawings (€)	1,500	1,500	1,500	1,500	1,500	1,500	9,000
	97,800	23,650	13,650	38,650	15,650	17,650	207,050
Opening Balance (€)	120,000	22,200	(1,450)	7,400	(3,750)	10,600	120,000
Net Cash (€)	(97,800)	(23,650)	8,850	(11,150)	14,350	12,350	(97,050)
Closing Balance (€)	22,200	(1,450)	7,400	(3,750)	10,600	22,950	22,950

Solution to Q 12.3(c)

Trading and Profit & Loss Accounts

	(€)	(€)	(€)
Sales (3,750 × 50)			187,500
Less Costs			
Opening Stock			
Purchases (4,100 × 20)		82,000	
Closing Stock (350 × 20)		7,000	
Cost of Sales			75,000
Gross profit			112,500
Less Expenses			
Wages		7,800	
Sundries (850 × 6)		5,100	
Depreciation: Premises	3,500		
Others	2,500	6,000	18,900
Net Profit			93,600

Balance Sheet

	Cost (€)	Depreciation (€)	Net (€)
Fixed Assets			
Premises	70,000	3,500	66,500
Others	50,000	2,500	47,500
	120,000	6,000	114,000
Less Current Assets			
Stock	7,000		
Debtors (2 months sales)	77,500		
Bank	22,950		
		107,450	
Less Current Liabilities			
Creditors (1 × Purchases)	16,000		
Expenses	850	16,850	90,600
			204,600
Financed by			
Capital	120,000		
Plus Net Profit	93,600		
	213,600		
Less Drawings	9,000		
			€204,600

Question 12.4

R Limited manufactures three products: A, B and C.

You are required, using the information given below, to prepare budgets for the month of January for

(a) sales in quantity and value, including total value,
(b) production quantities,
(c) material usage in quantities and
(d) material purchases in quantity and value, including total value.

(**Note:** Particular attention should be paid to your layout of the budgets.)

Data for Preparation of January Budgets

	Product	Quantity	Price Each (€)
Sales	A	1,000	100
	B	2,000	120
	C	1,500	140

Materials Used in the Company's Products

Material	M1	M2	M3
Unit Cost (€)	4	6	9

Quantities

Product	(units)	(units)	(units)
A	4	2	
B	3	3	2
C	2	1	1

Finished Stocks

	Product		
	A	B	C
Quantities			
1 January	1,000	1,500	500
31 January	1,100	1,650	550

Material stocks

	(units)	(units)	(units)
1 January	26,000	20,000	12,000
31 January	31,200	24,000	14,400

Solution to Q 12.4(a)

Sales Budget (Quantity & Value)

	Products		
	A	B	C
Sales Quantities (units)	1,000	2,000	1,500
Selling price (€ per unit)	100	120	140
Sales Value	€100,000	€240,000	€210,000
Total			€550,000

Solution to Q 12.4(b)

Production Budget (Quantities)

	Products		
	A	B	C
Sales (units) from Sales Budget	1,000	2,000	1,500
Add Closing Stock (units)	1,100	1,650	550
	2,100	3,650	2,050
Less Opening Stock (units)	1,000	1,500	500
Required Production	1,100	2,150	1,550

Solution to Q 12.4(c)

Material Usage Budget (Quantities)

		Materials					
		M1		M2		M3	
	Production Budget (Units)	Units per Product	Total	Units per Product	Total	Units per Product	Total
A	1,100	4	4,400	2	2,200		
B	2,150	3	6,450	3	6,450	2	4,300
C	1,550	2	3,100	1	1,550	1	1,550
Material Usage			13,950		10,200		5,850

Solution to Q 12.4(d)

Material Purchases Budget
(Quantities and Values)

	Materials			
	M1	M2	M3	
Usage from Budget (units)	13,950	10,200	5,850	
Add Closing Stock (units)	31,200	24,000	14,400	
	45,150	34,200	20,250	
Less Opening Stock (units)	26,000	20,000	12,000	
Equals Required Purchases (units)	19,150	14,200	8,250	
Unit Cost (€)	4	6	9	
Equals Value of Purchases (€)	76,600	85,200	74,250	
Total (€)				236,050

Question 12.5

Barnacarroll Plc requires you to prepare a month by month Cash Budget for the second half of 2001 based on the following information.

1. The company's only product sells at €60. It has a variable cost of €39 made up as follows: Labour €6, Material €30, Overheads €3.
2. Fixed Costs of €9,000 per month are paid on the last day of each month.
3. Credit Sales Quantities are as follows.

May	June	July	Aug	Sept	Oct	Nov	Dec
1,500	1,800	2,100	2,400	2,700	3,000	3,300	3,900

4. Production Quantities are as follows.

May	June	July	Aug	Sept	Oct	Nov	Dec
1,800	2,100	2,400	3,000	3,600	3,900	3,300	

5. Credit customers are to be given two months' credit.
6. Cash sales at a discount of 5 per cent are expected to average 200 units per month.
7. Suppliers of raw material give one month's credit.
8. Wages are paid in the month they are incurred.
9. The variable overhead is paid in the month following production.

Solution to Q 12.5

Credit Sales = Instruction 3 × €60 moved forward two months
Cash Sales = 200 × €60 – 5%

Barnacarroll Plc
Sales Budget Receipts

	July (€'000)	Aug (€'000)	Sept (€'000)	Oct (€'000)	Nov (€'000)	Dec (€'000)
Credit	90	108	126	144	162	180
Cash	11.4	11.4	11.4	11.4	11.4	11.4
Total **I**	101.4	119.4	137.4	155.4	173.4	191.4

Material = No. 4 × €30 plus one month
Wages = No. 4 × €6
Overhead = No. 4 × €3 plus one month

Payments

	July (€)	Aug (€)	Sept (€)	Oct (€)	Nov (€)	Dec (€)
Material	63	72	90	108	117	108
Wages	14.4	18	21.6	23.4	21.6	19.8
Overheads	6.3	7.2	9	10.8	11.7	10.8
Fixed	9	9	9	9	9	9
Total **II**	92.7	106.2	129.6	151.2	159.3	147.6
Net Cash **I – II**	8.7	13.2	7.8	3.2	14.1	43.8

Question 12.6

Planxty Limited manufacture a single product. Flexible budgets have been prepared below for activity levels of 70% and 100%.

Flexible Budgets

Activity Level	70%	100%
Units	7,000	10,000
	€	€
Direct Materials	42,000	60,000
Direct Labour	21,000	30,000
Production Overheads	31,000	37,000
Administration Overheads	28,000	28,000
Distribution Overheads	20,500	25,000
Total	142,500	180,000

Profit is 25% of Selling Price.

(a) Management has decided that a budget of 90% is required and that this should then be restated using Marginal Costing.

or

(b) The actual results were

Sales (8,000 units)	190,000
Materials	46,000
Labour	25,000
Production Overheads	32,000
Aministration Overheads	27,000
Distribution Overheads	22,000

Compare the budget with the actual.

Solution to Q 12.6

(i) Production Overheads

	€	Units
High	37,000	10,000
Low	31,000	7,000
	6,000	3,000

The Variable element is €2 per unit @ 10,000 = €20,000 variable, Total = €37,000 and Fixed = €17,000.

(ii) Distribution Overheads

	€	Units
High	25,000	10,000
Low	20,500	7,000
	4,500	3,000

The Variable element is €1.50 per unit @ 10,000 units = 15,000 Variable, Total = €25,000 and Fixed €10,000.

(iii) Flexible Budget @ 90%

		€
Direct Material	(9,000 × €6)	54,000
Direct Labour	(9,000 × €3)	27,000
Prodn. O/H	(9,000 × €2) + €17,000	35,000
Admin O/H		28,000
Distrib. O/H	(9,000 × €1.50) + €10,000	23,500
Total		167,500
Profit		58,333
Sales		225,833

(iv) Marginal Costing

Sales		225,833
Less Variable Costs		
Materials	54,000	
Labour	27,000	
Production O/H	18,000	
Distribution O/H	13,500	112,500
Contribution		113,333
Fixed Costs		
Production O/H	17,000	
Administration O/H	28,000	
Distribution O/H	10,000	55,000
Profit		58,333

or (b)

	80%	Actual	Variance	
Direct Material	48,000	46,000	2,000	F
Direct Labour	24,000	25,000	(1,000)	A
Production O/H	33,000	32,000	1,000	F
Administration O/H	28,000	27,000	1,000	F
Distribution O/H	22,000	22,000	–	
Total	155,000	152,000	3,000	F
Profit	51,667	38,000	(13,667)	A
Sales	206,667	190,000	(16,667)	A

Chapter 13

Farm Accounts

Agriculture is vital to our economy. Farming nowadays is a very complex business, subject to much outside regulation and rapid change. Information is vital to the farmer in arriving at decisions. Farm accounts should be prepared in such a way as to give maximum information.

1. Analyse as fully as possible each enterprise within the farm.
2. This may be done using separate accounts or using columnar accounts.
3. Allocate as many of the expenses as you can.
4. The other items may be unallocated or allocated, e.g. evenly, but explain what you are doing.
5. Dealing with Drawings and Capital Introduced will be the same as in incomplete records.
6. In valuing stocks, remember SSAP 9, and value at the lower of cost and net realisable value.

Question 13.1

The following is the Trial Balance of the Duggan family of Meadowbrook Farm who keep a complete set of double-entry accounts.

Trial Balance at 31 December 2001

	Debit (€)	Credit (€)
Stocks (1 January 2001)		
Livestock	80,000	
Feedstuffs	4,500	
Fertilisers	8,800	
Grain	21,600	
Purchases		
Livestock	38,000	
Feedstuffs	12,600	
Seeds	4,000	
Fertilisers	11,600	

Continued

Trial Balance *Continued*

	Debit (€)	Credit (€)
Milk Receipts		78,000
Sale of Livestock		62,000
Sale of Grain		58,000
Annual Grants		26,000
Electricity	3,800	
Subcontractors	8,800	
Repairs	3,600	
Veterinary Fees	1,960	
Wages	13,500	
Insurance	2,300	
Bank	1,700	
9% Farm Development Loan		60,000
Drawings	9,810	
Capital		270,570
Farm Land & Buildings (cost)	320,000	
Accumulated Depreciation Land & Buildings		10,000
Farm Machinery	42,000	
Accumulated Depreciation Farm Machinery		24,000
	588,570	588,570

The following information is also available.

1. Closing Stocks

	Cost (€)	Market Value (€)
Livestock	65,000	95,000
Grain	22,500	17,000
Feedstuffs	3,600	3,600
Fertilisers	7,600	7,400

2. Provide for a year's loan interest.
3. Provide depreciation at the rate of 20 per cent of cost per annum on farm machinery and 1 per cent of cost per annum on farm buildings (cost €120,000). Land is not depreciated.
4. Value of farm produce used by family is €4,000.
5. Allocate the following.

	Livestock & Milk (%)	Grain (%)
Wages	70	30
Subcontractors	40	60
Repairs	60	40
Others	50	50

6. Electricity due is €400.

Prepare in as much detail as possible

(a) the Enterprise and Final Accounts and
(b) the Balance Sheet.

Solution to Q 13.1(a)

Duggan Family/Meadowbrook Farm
Enterprise Analysis Accounts for the
Year Ended 31 December 2001

	Milk & Cattle (€)	Grain (€)
Sales (78,000 + 62,000)	140,000	58,000
Annual Grant	13,000	13,000
	153,000	71,000
Less Costs		
Opening Stock	80,000	21,600
Purchases	38,000	4,000
	118,000	25,600
Less Closing Stock	65,000	17,000
Cost	53,000	8,600
Electricity	2,100	2,100
Subcontractors	3,520	5,280
Repairs	2,160	1,440
Veterinary Fees	1,960	
Wages	9,450	4,050
Insurance	1,150	1,150
Loan Interest	2,700	2,700
Depreciation		
Machinery	4,200	4,200
Farm Buildings	600	600
Fertiliser	6,500	6,500
Feedstuffs	13,500	
	100,840	36,620
Profit	52,160	34,380

Note: All expenses have been allocated.

Farm Profit & Loss

	(€)
Profit on Milk & Livestock	52,160
Profit on Grain	34,380
Produce Used by Family	4,000
Total to Balance Sheet	90,540

Solution to Q 13.1(b)

Balance Sheet at 31 December 2001

	Cost (€)	Accumulated Depreciation (€)	Net Value (€)
Fixed Assets			
Land & Buildings	320,000	11,200	308,800
Machinery	42,000	32,400	9,600
	362,000	43,600	318,400
Current Assets			
Stocks: Livestock	65,000		
Grain	17,000		
Feedstuffs	3,600		
Fertilisers	7,400	93,000	
Bank		1,700	
		94,700	
Current Liabilities			
Loan Interest	5,400		
Electricity	400	5,800	
Net Current Assets			88,900
			407,300
Financed by			
Capital	270,570		
Plus Net Profit	90,540		
	361,110		
Less Drawings	13,810	347,300	
9% Farm Loan		60,000	
			€407,300

Question 13.2

Jimmy Tolan farms a mixed farming enterprise. He does not keep a full set of accounts and provides you with the following information for the year 2001.

He had the following assets and liabilities at 1 January 2001: Land & Buildings €230,000; Machinery €35,000; Stock of Cattle €60,000; Stock of Sheep €40,000; Stock of Feedstuffs €3,600; Electricity due €560; Insurance Prepaid €450 (3 months); Bank €6,800.

Note: All farm receipts are lodged and all payments are made by cheque.

His bank statements for the year reveal the following.

Lodgements: Sale of Cattle €110,000; Sale of Sheep €40,000; Headage & Premium Receipts €43,000.

Payments: Cattle €40,000; Sheep €60,000; Electricity €1,500; Diesel €1,800; Insurance (12 months) €2,000; Silage and Haymaking €16,300; Fertilisers €4,600; Drawings €15,000. Veterinary Fees €1,650; Casual labour €2,400; Interest €4,000; Loan Instalment €10,000.

On 1 July 2001 he borrowed €100,000, which was used to purchase some adjoining land. The rate of interest was to be 12 per cent payable monthly in arrears. The loan was to be repaid in ten equal instalments on 31 December each year.

One-quarter of the following are to be regarded as drawings: Insurance Paid, Electricity Used and Diesel Paid.

On 31 December he had the following Assets & Liabilities: Stock of Cattle €70,000; Stock of Sheep €50,000; Fertiliser €1,000; Feedstuffs €5,400; Electricity Bill due €480.

Prepare the Final Accounts for the year ended 31 December 2001 and a Balance Sheet at the same date.

Solution to Q 13.2

Jimmy Tolan Farmer
Capital

	Debit (€)	Credit (€)
1 January		
Land & Buildings	230,000	
Machinery	35,000	
Stock		
Cattle	60,000	
Sheep	40,000	
Feed	3,600	
Electricity Due		560
Insurance Prepaid	450	
Bank	6,800	
Capital		375,290
	375,850	375,850

Profit & Loss Account for Year Ended 31 December 2001

Sales			
Cattle		110,000	
Sheep		40,000	
Headage and Premium		43,000	193,000
Less Expenses			
Cattle Opening Stock	60,000		
Add Purchases	40,000		
	100,000		
Less Closing Stock	70,000	30,000	
Sheep Opening Stock	40,000		
Add Purchases	60,000		
	100,000		
Less Closing Stock	50,000	50,000	
OR if these are allocated show the following.			
Gross Profit: Cattle		80,000	
Gross Loss Sheep		(10,000)	
Headage, etc		43,000	
(but part of the Headage would be for sheep)			113,000
Foodstuffs (1 January)	3,600		
For Silage and Haymaking	16,300		
	19,900		
Less Feedstuffs (31 December)	5,400	14,500	
Fertiliser	4,600		
Less Stock (31 December)	1,000	3,600	
Veterinary Fees		1,650	
Casual Labour		2,400	
Interest		6,000	
Electricity		1,065	
Insurance		1,450	
Diesel		1,350	
			32,015
Net Profit			80,985

Electricity Account

	(€)		(€)
Bank	1,500	Balance	560
Balance	480	Drawings	355
		Profit & Loss	1,065
	1,980		1,980

Insurance Account

	(€)		(€)
Balance	450	Drawings	500
Bank	2,000	Profit & Loss	1,450
		Balance	500
	2,450		2,450

Diesel Account

	(€)		(€)
Bank	1,800	Drawings	450
		Profit & Loss	1,350
	1,800		1,800

Balance Sheet at 31 December 2001

	(€)	(€)	(€)
Fixed Assets			
Land & Buildings			330,000
Machinery			35,000
			365,000
Current Assets			
Stock: Cattle	70,000		
Sheep	50,000		
Fertiliser	1,000		
Feedstuffs	5,400		
Insurance Prepaid	500		
Bank	40,550		
		167,450	
Current Liabilities			
ESB Bill	480		
Interest	2,000		
	2,480	2,480	
Working Capital			164,970
			529,970
Financed by			
Capital		375,290	
Add Net Profit		80,985	
Less Drawings		(16,305)	439,970
Loan			90,000
			€529,970

Question 13.3
The following is the Trial Balance of a farmer, James Keogh, who keeps a complete set of double-entry accounts.

Trial Balance at 31 December 2000

	(€)	(€)
Farm Land & Buildings	250,000	
Farm Machinery at Cost	27,000	
Accumulative Depreciation — Farm Machinery		15,000
Stocks 1 January		
Livestock	70,000	
Grain	18,500	
Fertilisers	9,400	
Purchases		
Livestock	24,700	
Feeding Stuffs	7,600	
Seeds	3,900	
Fertilisers	21,250	
Sale of Grain		10,000
Sale of Cattle		39,300
Receipts from Creamery for Milk		27,750
Farm Wages	8,500	
Diesel Oil and Petrol	4,900	
Electricity	1,260	
Rates	3,440	
Repairs to Farm Machinery	725	
Veterinary Fees and Medicines	1,275	
Subcontractors for Harvesting	2,700	
Drawings	5,800	
Creditors for Fertilisers		3,900
Bank Overdraft		7,500
Bank Interest	1,300	
Capital		313,800
Loan from Agricultural Corporation		50,000
Loan Interest	5,000	
	467,250	467,250

The following additional information is available.

1. Closing Stocks.

	Cost (€)	Market Value (€)
Grain	30,000	40,000
Fertilisers	9,750	12,000
Cattle	120,000	125,000

2. Value of farm produce used by Keogh and family is €2,600.
3. Depreciation of farm machinery is computed at 10 per cent on cost.
4. The December cheque from the creamery amounting to €1,850 was not received until 20 January.
5. The amount of €4,000 is due to subcontractors for harvest work, and one-quarter of the rates has been paid in advance.
6. Farm wages and fertilisers should be allocated as one-half to cattle and milk and one-half to crops.
7. On 31 December, €5,000 due for rent from conacre had not yet been received.

Prepare

(a) Enterprise Analysis Accounts and
(b) Final Accounts and Balance Sheet at 31 December 2000.
(c) Advise James Keogh on whether his two major enterprises should be continued.

Solution to Q 13.3(a)

Enterprise Analysis Account of Cattle and Milk for the Year Ended 31 December 2000

	(€)		(€)
Opening Stock — Cattle	70,000	Sale of Cattle	39,300
Purchases	24,700	Sale of Milk	29,600
Feeding Stuffs	7,600	Closing Stock — Cattle	120,000
Wages	4,250		
Veterinary Fees	1,275		
Fertilisers	10,450		
Gross Profit transferred to Trading Account	70,625		
	188,900		188,900

Enterprise Analysis Account of Crops for the Year Ended 31 December 2000

	(€)		(€)
Opening Stock — Grain	18,500	Sale of Grain	10,000
Purchase of Seeds	3,900	Closing Stock of Grain	30,000
Fertilisers	10,450	Transferred to Trading	3,800
Wages	4,250		
Subcontractor for Harvesting	6,700		
	43,800		43,800

Solution to Q 13.3(b)

Trading Account for the Year Ended 31 December 2000

	(€)
Gross Profit on Cattle & Milk	70,625
Add Produce Used by Family	2,600
	73,225
Less Loss on Crops	3,800
Gross Profit Transferred to Profit & Loss Account	69,425

Profit & Loss Account for the Year Ended 31 December 2000

	(€)	(€)
Gross Profit from Trading Account		69,425
Add Rent due from Conacre		5,000
Less Expenses		
Diesel Oil & Petrol	4,900	
Electricity	1,260	
Rates	2,580	
Repairs to Farm Machinery	725	
Bank Interest	1,300	
Loan Interest	5,000	
Depreciation on Machinery	2,700	18,465
Net Profit		55,960

Balance Sheet at 31 December 2000

	Cost (€)	Accumulated Depreciation (€)	Book Value (€)
Fixed Assets			
Land & Buildings	250,000		250,000
Machinery	27,000	17,700	9,300
	277,000	17,700	259,300
Current Assets			
Stocks: Grain	30,000		
Cattle	120,000		

Continued

Balance Sheet at 31 December 2000 *Continued*

	Cost (€)	Accumulated Depreciation (€)	Book Value (€)
Fertilisers	9,750	159,750	
Debtor (Creamery)		1,850	
Rent Received Due		5,000	
Rates Prepaid		860	
		167,460	
Less Current Liabilities			
Creditors — Fertilisers	3,900		
Subcontractors	4,000		
Bank Overdraft	7,500	15,400	152,060
			411,360
Financed by			
Capital			313,800
Add Net Profit			55,960
			369,760
Less Drawings			8,400
			361,360
Long-Term Liabilities			
Loan from Agricultural Corporation			50,000
			411,360

Solution to Q 13.3(c)

He is losing money on his crops enterprise and this may be discontinued although farm enterprises which make a loss in one year may be profitable in another.

Chapter 14

Conceptual and Regulatory Framework

SSAPs stands for Statements of Standard Accounting Practice.

SSAP 2

SSAP 2 recognises four fundamental accounting concepts:

1. Going Concern
2. Consistency
3. Accruals
4. Prudence.

1 Going Concern

The accounts are prepared on the assumption that the business will continue into the future.

2 Consistency

Accounting items will be treated in the same way from one period to the next, e.g. depreciation of 20 per cent of cost will not be changed overnight to 30 per cent written-down value.

3 Accruals

'Accruals' is also a matching concept. Expenses for a period will be allocated to that period. Expenses for a period paid or unpaid must be included. Expenses prepaid will be excluded.

4 Prudence

'Prudence' is also known as the concept of conservatism. This says that losses should always be anticipated but not gains. Only realised gains should be taken into account. Always refer back to this concept.

SSAP 9. Stock

Stock is valued at the lower of cost and net realisable value. This is simply the concept of prudence restated. If stock goes down in value, it is the lower figure that should be used; but if it goes up in value, it should not be valued at the higher figure.

Government Regulation

Under the 1963 Companies Act, directors are responsible for preparing and presenting the accounts in proper format. The nature, role and qualifications of auditors are also clearly set out and will be explained more fully further on.

Under the 1986 Companies Act, which is an extension of the 1963 Act, the Fourth Directive of the EU was enacted. It sets out the format for presentation of the accounts. The Act classifies three types of companies, i.e. small, medium and large. It sets out three criteria for classification, all three of which must be attained.

Classification of Small and Medium Companies

Criteria	Small	Medium
1. Turnover	<€3M	>€3 and <€12M
2. Total of Balance Sheet	<€1.5M	>€1.5 and <€6M
3. Employees	<50	>50 and <250

Note: All other companies are large.

Full disclosure must be made by all public companies and large private companies. However, medium and small private companies need disclose less information. Information must be disclosed to the shareholders and the registrar of companies, i.e. filed.

Disclosure Requirements of Companies

	Public and Large Private		Medium Private		Small Private	
	Members	Filed	Members	Filed	Members	Filed
Profit & Loss	Full	Full	Short	Short	Short	None
Balance Sheet	Full	Full	Full	Abridged	Abridged	Abridged

Note: All must give a true and fair view.

The Auditors

'All auditors are accountants but not all accountants are auditors'.

The auditors are independent accountants who are appointed by the shareholders and can only be removed by shareholders.

It is the directors' function to prepare the accounts not the auditors'. The auditors report on the preparation of the accounts by the directors to the shareholders in standard format annually. This will be 'unqualified' or 'qualified'. An unqualified report gives the shareholders assurance as to the accuracy of the accounts. If the auditors are not satisfied, they must state this in the form of a qualified report.

If the auditors discover fraud, they must report it, although the detection of fraud is not their primary function. The audit should be conducted with due care and diligence.

LEAVING CERTIFICATE ACCOUNTING

MARKING SCHEME FOR THE EXAMINATION

The solutions are printed and the marks allocated to each line/figure are highlighted and shown in a circle like this ❻. These marks are then totalled for each section/page and shown in a square like this **40**.

Accounting solutions are mainly computational and most figures are made up of more than one component. If a figure is wrong for the solution, the examiners analyse the make-up of the candidate's figure and allocate some marks for each correct element included. To facilitate this, where relevant, the make-up of the figures is shown in workings attached to the solution.

In some Accounting questions there can be a number of alternative approaches and formats that can be validly used by candidates (e.g. a Bank Reconciliation Statement can start with either the bank statement figure or the adjusted bank account balance). The solutions provided here are based on the approaches adopted by the vast majority of teachers/candidates and alternatives are not included. In cases where a valid alternative solution is required, it is provided for the examiners, so that full marks can be gained for correct accounting treatment.

Sometimes the solution to a part of a question may depend on the answer computed in another part of that question. Where the calculation in Section (a) is incorrect, but this inaccurate information is used in the answer to Section (b), examiners give credit for analysis/decisions correctly made by the candidate on the basis of the incorrect data in this section. In this way, candidates are not penalised twice for the same error.

LEAVING CERTIFICATE EXAMINATION, 2004

Accounting – Higher Level

(400 marks)

9.30 a.m. to 12.30 p.m.

This paper is divided into 3 Sections:

Section 1: Financial Accounting (120 marks)

This section has 4 questions (Numbers 1–4). The first question carries 120 marks and the remaining three questions carry 60 marks each.
Candidates should answer either **QUESTION 1 only** OR else attempt any **TWO** of the remaining three questions in this section.

Section 2: Financial Accounting (200 marks)

This section has three questions (Numbers 5–7). Each question carries 100 marks.
Candidates should answer any **TWO** questions.

Section 3: Management Accounting (80 marks)

This section has two questions (Numbers 8 and 9). Each question carries 80 marks.
Candidates should answer **ONE** of these questions.

Calculators

Calculators may be used in answering the questions on this paper: however, it is very important that workings are shown in the answer book(s) so that full credit can be given for correct work.

SECTION 1 (120 marks)

Answer **QUESTION 1** OR any **TWO** other questions

---

1. **Company Final Accounts**

Carey Ltd has an Authorised capital of €990,000 divided into 690,000 Ordinary shares at €1 each and 300,000 7% Preference shares at €1 each. The following Trial Balance was extracted from its books on 31/12/2003.

	€	€
Land and building at cost	780,000	
Accumulated depreciation – Land and buildings		39,000
Patents (incorporating 2 months' investment income received)	58,200	
6% Investments 1/5/2003	180,000	
Delivery vans at cost	172,000	
Accumulated depreciation – Delivery vans		78,000
Stocks 1/1/2003	76,600	
Purchases and sales	620,000	990,000
Directors' fees	80,000	
Salaries and general expenses	176,000	
Debenture interest paid	4,500	
Profit and loss balance 1/1/2003		67,600
Debtors and Creditors	73,900	81,000
Provision for bad debts		3,600
Interim dividends for first 6 months	40,000	
9% Debentures (including €80,000 9% debentures issued at par on 31/3/2003)		230,000
VAT		16,500
Bank		5,500
Issued capital		
550,000 Ordinary shares at €1 each		550,000
200,000 7% Preference shares €1 each		200,000
	2,261,200	2,261,200

The following information and instructions are to be taken into account:

(i) Stock at 31/12/2003 at cost was €85,000 – this figure includes old stock which cost €8,000 but has a net realisable value of 60% of cost.

(ii) Patents, which incorporated 2 months' investment income, are to be written off over a 5 year period commencing in 2003.

(iii) Provide for depreciation on delivery vans at the annual rate of 20% of cost from the date of purchase to the date of sale.

NOTE: On 31/9/2003 a delivery van, which had cost €60,000 on 1/6/2001, was traded in against a new van which cost €84,000. An allowance of €22,000 was given on the old van. The cheque for the net amount of this transaction was incorrectly treated as a purchase of trading stock. This was the only entry made in the books in respect of this transaction.

(iv) Buildings are to be depreciated at the rate of 2% of cost per annum (land at cost was €130,000). At the end of 2003 the company re-valued the Land and buildings at €880,000.

(v) The figure for bank in the trial balance has been taken from the firm's bank account. However, a bank statement dated 31/12/2003 has arrived showing a credit balance of €4,040. A comparison of the bank account and the bank statement has revealed the following discrepancies:

1. Investment income €2,700 had been paid direct to the firm's bank account.
2. A cheque for €780, issued to a supplier, had been entered in the books (cash *book* and ledger) as €870.
3. A credit transfer of €750 had been paid direct to the firm's bank account on behalf of a debtor who has recently been declared bankrupt. This represents a first and final payment of 30c in the €1.
4. A cheque for fees €6,000 issued to a director had not yet been presented for payment.

(vi) The directors recommend that:

1. The Preference dividend due be paid.
2. A final dividend on Ordinary shares be provided bringing the total dividend up to 9c per share.
3. Provision be made for both Investment income and Debenture interest due.
4. Provision for bad debts be adjusted to 4% of debtors.

You are required to prepare a:

(a) Trading and Profit and loss account, for the year ended 31/12/2003. (75)

(b) Balance sheet as at 31/12/2003. (45)

(120 marks)

2. Tabular Statement

The financial position of Casey Ltd on 1/1/2003 is shown in the following Balance sheet:

Balance sheet as at 1/1/2003

	Cost €	Dep. to date €	Net €
Fixed Assets			
Land & buildings	460,000	13,800	446,200
Delivery vans	76,000	33,000	43,000
	536,000	46,800	489,200
Current Assets			
Stock	59,800		
Insurance prepaid	1,500		
Debtors	61,700	123,000	
Less Creditors: amount falling due within 1 year			
Creditors	62,500		
Bank	10,100		
Wages due	2,400	75,000	
Net Current Assets			48,000
			537,200
Financed by			
Capital and reserves			
Authorised – 850,000 Ordinary shares @ €1 each			
Issued – 430,000 Ordinary shares @ €1 each		430,000	
Share premium		40,000	
Profit and loss balance		67,200	
			537,200

The following transactions took place during 2003:

Jan — Casey Ltd decided to re-value the Land and buildings at €580,000 on 1/1/2003, which includes land now valued at €100,000.

Feb — On 1/02/03 Casey Ltd bought an adjoining business which included Buildings €360,000, Delivery vans €58,000, Stock €25,000 and Creditors €33,000. The purchase price was discharged by granting the seller 400,000 shares in Casey Ltd at a premium of 20c per share.

March — Goods, previously sold by Casey Ltd for €1,800, were returned. The selling price of these goods was cost plus 20%. Owing to the delay in returning these goods a credit note was issued showing a deduction of 10% of invoice price as a restocking charge.

April A delivery van which cost €20,000 was traded-in against a new van costing €36,000. An allowance of €12,500 was made for the old van. Depreciation to date on the old van was €6,600.

May Received a bank statement on May 31 showing a direct debit of €4,800 to cover fire insurance for year ended 31/5/2004.

July A payment of €720 was received from a debtor whose debt had been previously written off and who now wishes to trade with Casey Ltd again. This represents 60% of the original debt and the debtor had undertaken to pay the remainder of the debt in January 2004.

Dec The Buildings depreciation charge for the year to be 2% of book value. The depreciation charge to be calculated from date of valuation and date of purchase. The total depreciation charge on delivery vans for the year was €22,000.

You are required to:

Record on a tabular statement the effect each of the above transactions had on the relevant asset and liability and ascertain the total assets and liabilities on 31/12/2003.

(60 marks)

3. Revaluation of Fixed Assets

On 1 January 1999 Cavanagh Ltd owned freehold property and land which cost €740,000, consisting of Land €250,000 and Buildings €490,000. The company depreciates its buildings at the rate of 2% per annum using the straight line method. It is the company's policy to apply a full year's depreciation in the year of acquisition and no depreciation in the year of disposal. This property had been purchased ten years earlier and depreciation had been charged against profits in each of these ten years (Land is not depreciated).

The following details were taken from the firm's books:

Jan 1 1999 Re-valued property at €870,000. Of this revaluation €300,000 was attributable to land.

Jan 1 2000 Sold for €330,000 land which cost €250,000 but was since re-valued on 1/1/1999

Jan 1 2001 Purchased buildings for €450,000. During the year 2001, €120,000 was paid to a building contractor for an extension to these recently purchased buildings. The company's own employees also worked on the extension and they were paid wages amounting to €60,000 by Cavanagh Ltd for this work.

Jan 1 2002 Re-valued buildings owned at €1,320,000 (a 10% increase in respect of each building).

Jan 1 2003 Sold for €700,000 the buildings owned on 1/1/1999. The remaining buildings were re-valued at €800,000.

You are required to:

Prepare the relevant ledger accounts in respect of the above transactions for the years ended 31 December 1999 to 31 December 2003 **(Bank Account and Profit and Loss Account *not* required).**

(60 marks)

4. Cash Flow Statement

The following are the balance sheets of Creation Plc as at 31/12/2002 and 31/12/2003, together with an abridged profit and loss account for the year ended 31/12/2003:

Abridged Profit and Loss Account for the year ended 31/12/2003		€
Operating profit		150,600
Interest for year		(10,600)
Profit before taxation		140,000
Taxation for year		(47,000)
Profit after taxation		93,000
Dividends – Interim	23,000	
– Proposed	48,000	(71,000)
Retained profits for the year		22,000
Retained profits on 1/1/2003		189,000
Retained profits on 31/12/2003		211,000

Balance Sheets as at	**31/12/2003**		**31/12/2002**	
Fixed Assets	€	€	€	€
Land and buildings at cost	800,000		725,000	
Less accumulated depreciation	(75,000)	725,000	(60,000)	665,000
Machinery at cost	380,000		450,000	
Less accumulated depreciation	(190,000)	190,000	(170,000)	280,000
		915,000		945,000
Financial Assets				
Quoted investments		120,000		90,000
Current Assets				
Stock	225,000		208,000	
Debtors	212,000		184,000	
Bank	–		12,000	
Cash	3,000		1,000	
	440,000		405,000	
Less **Creditors: amounts falling due within 1 year**				
Trade creditors	253,000		230,000	
Interest due	1,400		–	
Taxation	51,000		44,000	
Dividends	48,000		37,000	
Bank	8,600		–	
	(362,000)		(311,000)	
Net Current Assets		78,000		94,000
		1,113,000		1,129,000

Financed by				
Creditors: amounts falling due after more than 1 year				
8% Debentures		50,000		160,000
Capital and Reserves				
€1 Ordinary shares	840,000		780,000	
Share premium	12,000		–	
Profit and loss account	211,000	1,063,000	189,000	969,000
		1,113,000		1,129,000

The following information is also available:

1. There were no disposals of buildings during the year but new buildings were acquired.
2. There were no purchases of machinery during the year. Machinery was disposed of for €24,000.
3. Depreciation charged for the year on machinery in arriving at the operating profit was €55,000.

You are required to:

(a) Reconcile the operating profit to net cash inflow from operating activities. (20)

(b) Prepare the cash flow statement of Creation Plc for the year ended 31/12/2003. (30)

(c) Explain why profit does not always mean a corresponding increase in cash and list two non cash items. (10)

(60 marks)

SECTION 2 (200 marks)

Answer **TWO** other questions

5. Interpretation of Accounts

The following figures have been extracted from the final accounts of Coulter Ltd, a service provider in the leisure industry, whose Authorised Capital is €900,000, made up of 650,000 Ordinary Shares at €1 each and 250,000 10% Preference Shares.

Trading and Profit and Loss account for year ended 31/12/2003

		€
Sales		1,100,000
Costs of goods sold		
Stock 1/1/2003	63,000	
Purchases	751,000	
Stock 31/12/2003	(74,000)	(740,000)
Total operating expenses for the year		(208,000)
Interest for year		(15,000)
Net Profit for year		137,000
Proposed dividends		(66,000)
Retained profits for year		71,000

Ratios and figures for year ended 31/12/2002

Earnings per ordinary share	22c
Dividend per ordinary share	2.9c
Quick ratio	0.9 to 1
Market value of ordinary share	€1.75
Return on capital employed	14%
Return on equity funds	19%
Interest cover	9 times
Gearing	40%

Balance Sheet as at 31/12/2003

Intangible Assets	140,000	
Fixed Assets	760,000	900,000
Current Assets	170,000	
Current Liabilities		
Trade creditors	(35,000)	
Proposed dividends	(66,000)	69,000
		969,000
9% Debentures 2008/2009		160,000
Issued capital		
500,000 Ordinary shares @ €1 each	500,000	
200,000 10% preference shares @ €1 each	200,000	
Profit and loss balance	119,000	839,000
		969,000

You are required to answer the following:

(a) (i) Cash purchases if the average period of credit received from creditors is 1.5 months.

(ii) Earnings per share.

(iii) How long it would take one ordinary share to recoup (recover) its 2002 market price based on present dividend payout rate.

(iv) The dividend yield for **2002**.

(v) The market value of one ordinary share **in 2003** if the price earnings ratio is 9.

(50)

(b) Assume that the company wishes to raise further finance by issuing the remaining shares at €2 per share. Would you as a shareholder be prepared to purchase these shares? Outline your reasons for purchasing/not purchasing some shares. Your answer should include all relevant information included in the above figures and references to any other information that you consider necessary. (50)

(100 marks)

6. Club Accounts

Included among the assets and liabilities of the Green Glen Golf Club on 1/1/2003 were the following: Clubhouse & course €740,000, Bar stock €3,800, Equipment (at cost) €28,600, Life membership €36,000, Bar debtors €155, Bar creditors €2,450, Subscriptions received in advance €1,800, 6% Government investments €40,000, Investment income due €150, Levy reserve fund €60,000 and Wages due €2,400.

The Club Treasurer has supplied the following account of the Club's activities during the year ended 31/12/2003:

Receipts	**€**	**Payments**	**€**
Bank Current Account	4,440	Bar purchases	80,500
Investment income	1,450	Sundry expenses	185,600
Entrance fees	17,000	Catering costs	4,460
Catering receipts	6,650	Equipment	44,500
Annual sponsorship	33,000	Coaching lessons	4,650
Subscriptions	254,200	Repayment of €30,000 loan on 31/12/2003 together with $1^1/_4$ years' interest	34,500
Bar receipts	112,660	Transfer to Building Society 31/12/2003	70,000
		Balance	5,190
	€429,400		€429,400

You are given the following additional information and instructions:

1. Bar stock on 31/12/2003 was €4,300.
2. Equipment owned on 31/12/2003 is to be depreciated at the rate of 20% of cost.
3. Clubhouse and course to be depreciated by 2% of cost.
4. Bar debtors and bar creditors on 31/12/2003 were €110 and €2,770 respectively.
5. Subscriptions include:
   - 2 life memberships of €6,000 each.
   - Subscriptions for 2004 amounting to €2,400.
   - Levy for 2003 of €200 on 300 members.
   - Levy of €200 on 8 members for 2002.
6. Life membership was to be written off over a 12 year period commencing in 2003.

You are required to:

(a) Show the Club's accumulated fund (capital) on 1/1/2003. (30)

(b) Show the Income and Expenditure Account for the year ended 31/12/2003. (35)

(c) Show the Club's Balance Sheet on 31/12/2003. (20)

(d) Indicate the points you, as treasurer, might make if the members at the AGM of the club proposed to reduce the annual subscription by 20%. (15)

(100 marks)

7. Correction of errors and suspense account

The Trial Balance of S. Craddock, a furniture and carpet trader, failed to agree on 31/12/2003. The difference was entered in a Suspense Account and the following Balance Sheet was prepared.

Balance Sheet as at 31/12/2003

		€	€
Fixed Assets			
Premises		650,000	
Fixtures & fittings		72,000	722,000
Current Assets			
Stock (including suspense)		88,600	
Debtors		33,300	
Cash		400	
		122,300	
Less: Current Liabilities			
Creditors	52,000		
Bank	27,000	79,000	43,300
			765,300
Financed by:			
Capital		730,000	
Add: Net profit		63,300	
		793,300	
Less: Drawings		28,000	765,300
			765,300

On checking the books, the following errors were discovered:

(i) Furniture, purchased on credit from J. Dolan for €16,500, had been entered as €6,500 on the incorrect side of Dolan's account and credited as €1,650 in the Fixtures & Fittings account.

(ii) A debtor who owed Craddock €900 sent a cheque for €750 and €100 in cash in full settlement. This was correctly recorded in the books. However, no entry had been made in the books of the subsequent dishonouring of this cheque or of the writing off of the remaining debt in full because of bankruptcy.

(iii) Bedside Lockers previously sold on credit for €340 had been returned to Craddock. These goods had been incorrectly entered as €34 on the credit of the Fixtures & fittings account and as €40 on the debit of the Purchases account.

(iv) A private debt for €1,600, owed by Craddock, had been offset in full against a business debt of €1,700, owed to the firm for carpet repairs previously carried out. No entry had been made in the books in respect of this offset.

(v) Craddock had returned furniture, previously purchased on credit from a supplier for €8,800, and had entered this transaction in the relevant ledger accounts incorrectly as €8,880. However, a credit note subsequently arrived from the supplier in respect of the return showing a transport charge of €200 to cover the cost of the return. The only entry made in respect of this credit note was a credit of €8,600 in the creditor's account.

You are required to:

(a) Journalise the necessary corrections. (55)

(b) Show the Suspense Account. (10)

(c) Prepare a Statement showing the correct net profit. (15)

(d) Prepare a corrected Balance Sheet. (20)

(100 marks)

SECTION 3 (80 marks)

Answer **ONE** question

8. Marginal Costing

Carroll Ltd produces a single product. The company's profit and loss account for the year ended 31/12/2003, during which 60,000 units were produced and sold, was as follows:

	€	€
Sales (60,000 units)		960,000
Materials	331,000	
Direct labour	158,300	
Factory overheads	81,000	
Administration expenses	113,400	
Selling expenses	78,000	761,700
Net profit		198,300

The materials, direct labour and 30% of the factory overheads are variable costs. Apart from the sales commission of €0.70 per unit, selling and administration expenses are fixed.

You are required to calculate:

(a) The company's break-even point and margin of safety.

(b) The number of units that must be sold in 2004 if the company is to increase its net profit by 15% over the 2003 figure assuming the selling price and cost levels and percentages remain unchanged.

(c) The profit the company would make in 2004 if it reduced its selling price to €14, increased fixed costs by €14,000 and thereby increased the number of units sold to 75,000, with all other cost levels and percentages remaining unchanged.

(d) The selling price the company must charge per unit in 2004, if fixed costs increase by 10% but the volume of sales and the profit remain the same.

(e) The number of units that must be sold at €17 per unit to provide a profit of 10% of the sales revenue received from these same units.

(f) List and explain two limitations/assumptions of marginal costing.

(80 marks)

9. Cash Budgeting

Slaney Ltd is preparing to set up business on 1/7/2004 and has made the following forecast for the first six months of trading:

	July	August	September	October	November	December	Total
Sales	€525,000	588,000	616,000	630,000	658,000	672,000	3,689,000
Purchases	€300,000	336,000	352,000	360,000	376,000	384,000	2,108,000

The expected selling price is €70 per unit.
The cash collection pattern from debtors is expected to be:

Cash customers – 30% of sales revenue will be for immediate cash and cash discount of 5% will be allowed.

Credit customers – 70% of sales revenue will be from credit customers. These creditors will pay their bills 50% in month after sale and the remainder in the second month after sale.

The purchases will be paid for 50% in month after purchase when 2% cash discount will be received. The remaining purchases will be paid for in the second month after purchase.

Expected costs: Wages €45,000 per month payable as incurred.
Variable overheads €10 per unit payable as incurred.
Fixed overheads (including depreciation) €52,000 per month payable as incurred.

Equipment will be purchased in July costing €48,000 which will have a useful life of 5 years. To finance this purchase a loan of €50,000 will be secured at the rate of 10% per annum. Interest to be paid monthly, but capital loan repayments will not commence until January 2005.

You are required to:

(a) Prepare a cash budget for six months July to December 2004.

(b) Prepare a budgeted profit and loss account for the six months ended 31/12/2004.

(80 marks)

Accounting – Higher Level 2004

Solutions

Question 1 75

(a) Trading, Profit and Loss Account for the year ended 31/12/2003

		€	€	€
Sales				990,000 ❷
Less Cost of sales				
Stock 1/1/2003			76,600 ❷	
Add Purchases	W 1		558,000 ❺	
			634,600	
Less Stock 31/12/2003	W 2		(81,800) ❺	(552,800)
Gross profit				437,200
Less Expenses				
Administration				
Directors' fees		80,000 ❷		
Salaries & general expenses		176,000 ❷		
Patents written off	W 3	12,000 ❻		
Depreciation – buildings	W 4	13,000 ❹	281,000	
Selling and Distribution				
Bad debts written off		1,750 ❹		
Depreciation – delivery vans	W 5	35,600 ❻		
Loss on sale of van	W 7	10,000 ❺	47,350	328,350
Operating profit				108,850
Decrease in provision for bad debts	W 6		744 ❺	
Investment income	W 8		7,200 ❹	7,944
				116,794
Debenture interest				(18,900) ❺
Net profit for year before taxation				97,894
Less Appropriation				
Preference dividend paid			7,000 ❷	
Ordinary dividend paid			33,000 ❸	
Preference dividend proposed			7,000 ❷	
Ordinary dividend proposed			16,500 ❸	(63,500)
Retained profit				34,394
Profit and loss balance 1/1/2003				67,600 ❷
Profit and loss balance 31/12/2003				101,994 ❻

Workings

1. Purchases	620,000 – 62,000	558,000
2. Closing stock	85,000 – 3,200	81,800
3. Patents written off	(€58,200 + €1,800) × 20%	12,000
4. Depreciation – buildings	2% of (780,000 – 130,000)	13,000
5. Depreciation – delivery vans	25,800 + 9,800	35,600
	34,400 + 1,200	35,600
	22,400 + 9,000 + 4,200	35,600
6. Decrease in Provision for bad debts	3,600 – 2,856	744
7. Loss on sale of van	60,000 – 22,000 – 28,000	10,000
8. Investment Income	1,800 + 2,700 + 2,700	7,200
9. Land and Buildings at cost	780,000 + 100,000	880,000
10. Delivery vans at cost	172,000 + 84,000 – 60,000	196,000
Accumulated Depreciation D. Vans	78,000 + 35,600 – 28,000	85,600
11. Debtors	73,900 – 750 – 1,750	71,400
12. Creditors	81,000 + 90	81,090
13. Bank overdraft as per Trial Balance	5,500	
Less Investment income	(2,700)	
Less Credit transfer received	(750)	
Less Bank under credited	(90)	(1,960)
Alternative	(4,040 – 6,000)	(1,960)
14. Revaluation reserve	100,000 + 39,000 + 13,000	152,000

Question 2

60

	1/1/2003 €	January €	February €	March €	April €	May €	July €	December €	Total €
Assets									
Land and Buildings	460,000	120,000 ❷	360,000 ❷						940,000
Accumulated Depreciation	(13,800)	13,800 ❷						(16,200) ❷	(16,200)
Delivery Vans	76,000		58,000 ❷		16,000 ❷				150,000
Accumulated Depreciation	(33,000)				6,600 ❷			(22,000) ❶	(48,400)
Stock	59,800		25,000 ❷	1,500 ❸					86,300
Debtors	61,700			(1,620) ❷			480 ❸		60,560
Insurance A/c (Prepaid)	1,500					4,800 ❸		(4,300) ❶	2,000 ❶
Goodwill			70,000 ❸						70,000
TOTAL	**612,200**	**133,800**	**513,000**	**(120)**	**22,600**	**4,800**	**480**	**(42,500)**	**1,244,260** ❶
Liabilities									
Share Capital	430,000		400,000 ❷						830,000
Share Premium	40,000		80,000 ❷						120,000
Revaluation Reserve		133,800 ❸							133,800
Profit and Loss	67,200			(120) ❶	(900) ❸		1,200 ❷	(42,500) ❸	24,880 ❷
Creditors	62,500		33,000 ❷						95,500
Wages due	2,400								2,400
Bank	10,100				23,500 ❶	4,800 ❷	(720) ❶		37,680 ❶
TOTAL	**612,200**	**133,800**	**513,000**	**(120)**	**22,600**	**4,800**	**480**	**(42,500)**	**1,244,260** ❶

Question 3

20

(a) Land and Buildings Account

Date	Details	€		Date	Details	€	
1/1/99	Balance b/d	740,000	2	31/12/99	Balance c/d	870,000	
1/1/99	Revaluation Res.	130,000	2				
		870,000				870,000	
1/1/00	Balance b/d	870,000		01/02/00	Disposal	300,000	1
				31/12/00	Balance c/d	570,000	
		870,000				870,000	
1/1/01	Balance b/d	570,000	1	31/12/01	Balance c/d	1,200,000	
	Bank	450,000	2				
	Bank	120,000	2				
	Wages	60,000	2				
		1,200,000				1,200,000	
1/1/02	Balance b/d	1,200,000		31/12/02	Balance c/d	1,320,000	
1/1/02	Revaluation Res	120,000	2				
		1,320,000				1,320,000	
1/1/03	Balance b/d	1,320,000		01/02/03	Disposal	627,000	3
1/1/03	Revaluation Res	107,000	3	31/12/03	Balance c/d	800,000	
		1,427,000				1,427,000	

23

Provision for Depreciation on Buildings Account

Date	Details	€		Date	Details	€	
1/1/99	Revaluation Res.	98,000	2	1/1/99	Balance b/d	98,000	4
31/12/99	Balance c/d	11,400		31/12/99	Profit and Loss	11,400	2
		109,400				109,400	
31/12/00	Balance c/d	22,800		1/1/00	Balance b/d	11,400	
				31/12/00	Profit and Loss	11,400	2
		22,800				22,800	
31/12/01	Balance c/d	46,800		1/1/01	Balance b/d	22,800	
				31/12/01	Profit and Loss	24,000	2
		46,800				46,800	
1/1/02	Revaluation Res.	46,800	2	1/1/02	Balance c/d	46,800	
31/12/02	Balance c/d	26,400		31/12/02	Profit and Loss	26,400	2
		73,200				73,200	
1/1/03	Disposal	12,540	2	1/1/03	Balance b/d	26,400	
1/1/03	Revaluation Res.	13,860	3	31/12/03	Profit and Loss	16,000	2
31/12/03	Balance c/d	16,000					
		42,400				42,400	
				1/1/03	Balance b/d	16,000	

Disposal of Land Account 3

		€			€
1/1/00	Buildings	300,000 ❶	1/1/00	Bank	330,000 ❶
31/12/00	P & L (Profit)	30,000 ❶			
		330,000			330,000

Disposal of Buildings Account 4

		€			€
1/1/03	Buildings	627,000 ❶	1/1/03	Depreciation	12,540 ❶
31/12/03	P & L (Profit)	85,540 ❶	1/1/03	Bank	700,000 ❶
		712,540			712,540

Revaluation Reserve Account 8

		€			€
1/1/99	Revenue reserve	50,000 ❶	1/1/99	Land and Buildings	130,000 ❶
1/1/03	Revenue reserve	269,200 ❶		Provision for Dep	98,000 ❶
	Balance	196,460	1/1/02	Land and Buildings	120,000 ❶
				Provision for Dep	46,800 ❶
			1/1/03	Land and Buildings	107,000 ❶
				Provision for Dep	13,860
		515,660			515,660

Revenue Reserve Account 2

		€			€
			1/1/99	Revenue reserve	50,000 ❶
			1/1/03	Revenue reserve	269,200 ❶

Question 4

(a) Reconciliation of operating profit to net cash flow from operating activities: **20**

		€	
Operating profit		150,600	2
Depreciation charges for year	W 1	70,000	4
Loss on sale of machinery	W 2	11,000	6
Increase in stocks		(17,000)	2
Increase in debtors		(28,000)	2
Increase in creditors		23,000	2
Net cash inflow from operating activities		209,600	2

(b) Cash Flow Statement of Creation Plc for the year ended 31/12/2003 **30**

				€	
Operating Activities					
Net cash inflow from operating activities				209,600	1
Returns on investments and servicing of finance 1					
Interest paid				(9,200)	3
Taxation 1					
Corporation tax paid				(40,000)	3
Capital expenditure and financial investment 1					
Investments		(30,000)	2		
Payments to acquire tangible fixed assets		(75,000)	2		
Receipts from sale of fixed assets		24,000	2	(81,000)	
Equity dividends paid 1					
Dividends paid during year	W 3			(60,000)	4
Net cash **inflow** before liquid resources and financing				19,400	
Financing					
Repayment of debentures		(110,000)	2		
Receipts from issue of shares		60,000	1		
Receipts from share premium		12,000	1	(38,000)	
Decrease in cash	2			**(18,600)**	

Reconciliation of net cash flow to movement in net debt	€	
Decrease in cash during period	(18,600)	1
Cash used to purchase debentures	110,000	1
Change in net debt	91,400	
Net debt at 1/1/2003	(147,000)	
Net debt at 31/12/2003	55,600	1

10

(c) Credit sales/purchases affect profit but do not affect cash

Non-cash losses and gains affect profit but not cash

Purchase and sale of fixed assets by cash affect cash but not profit

Introduction or withdrawal of capital in cash affect cash but not profit

Non-cash items – Depreciation, Provisions against losses, losses/profits from sale of assets

N.B. The three marks applied to Reconciliation Statement above are applied to 'Net **cash inflow** before financing €19,400' if old method was presented by candidates.

Headings 4 × 1 mark

Question 5

50

(a)

Cash purchases	$\frac{\text{Creditors} \times 12}{\text{Credit purchases}}$	= 1.5 Credit purchases = $\frac{35{,}000 \times 12}{1.5}$	
	Credit purchases	= 280,000	
	Cash purchases	= 751,000 – 280,000	= €471,000 ⓬
Earnings per share	$\frac{\text{Net profit after Pref Div} \times 100}{\text{Number of ordinary shares}}$	= $\frac{117{,}000 \times 100}{500{,}000}$	= 23.4c ❿
Period to recover price	$\frac{\text{Market Price}}{\text{Dividend per share}}$	= $\frac{175}{9.2}$	= 19 years ⓬
Dividend yield	$\frac{\text{Dividend per Ordinary Share} \times 100}{\text{Market Price}}$	= $\frac{2.9 \times 100}{1.75}$	= 1.66% ❽
Price earnings Ratio	$\frac{\text{Market Price}}{\text{Earnings per share}} = 9$	= $\frac{\text{Market Price}}{23.4}$ = 9	210.6c ❽

(b) **50**

Dividends ⑩

	2003	**2002**
Dividend per share	92c	2.9c
Dividend Yield	4.37%	1.66%
Dividend Cover in 2002 was	2.5 times	7.6 times
Real return – Div Yield × Div Cover	10.9%	12.6%

The dividend policy of company has eased over the two years as the percentage of profits paid out has increased from 13.15% to 40%.
The real return of 10.9% and 12.6% are well above the return from risk free investments of less than 5%.

Market Value of Share ❽
The market value of each share increased from €1.75 in 2002 to €2.11 in 2003.
The shares are now being offered at €2.00. This is 11c above 2003 value.
The price earnings ratio 2003 is 9 and 8 in 2002.

Profitability ❽
The Return on Shareholders equity increased from 19% in 2002 to 19.2% in 2003.
The Return on Capital Employed increased from 14% in 2002 to 15.7% in 2003.
This indicates a healthy trend and the value of share would further increase if this trend continues.
The return is better than the return from risk free investments of less than 5%.

Proportion of shares owned ❻
The remaining 150,000 shares would give the purchaser 23% ownership of the company. This amount added to shares already owned would bring the owner's shareholding close to the point of having to bid for the remainder of the shares.

Liquidity ❻
The Acid test ratio improved from 0.9 to 0.95. This is a satisfactory position as the company now has 95c available to pay each €1 owed in the short term.
The company does not have a liquidity problem.

Gearing ❻
The firm is low geared. The gearing has improved from 40% in 2002 to 37% of total capital in 2003. Interest Cover in 2002 was 9 times and this cover has increased to 10 times in 2003. This indicates that there is little risk from creditors and a better prospect of higher dividends.

Sector ❻
The Leisure industry is a growth industry. People are prepared to spend more of their disposable income on leisure.

Question 6 **30**

(a)

Accumulated Fund at 1 January 2003

	€		€	
Assets				
Clubhouse and Course	740,000	❶		
Bar stock	3,800	❶		
Equipment	28,600	❶		
Bar debtors	155	❶		
6% Government Investments	40,000	❷		
Interest on Investments	150	❷		
Levy due	1,600	❸		
Bank Current Account	4,440	❸	818,745	
Less Liabilities				
Life Membership	36,000	❷		
Creditors	2,450	❶		
Subscriptions prepaid	1,800	❷		
Levy Reserve Fund	60,000	❷		
Wages due	2,400	❶		
Loan	30,000	❷		
Loan interest due	900	❸	133,550	
Accumulated fund/Capital at 1 January 2003 ❶			685,195	❷

(b) **35**

Income and Expenditure Account for the year ended 31 December 2003

		€		€	
Income					
Bar profit	**W 1**	32,295	❻		
Investment income	**W 2**	2,400	❸		
Subscriptions	**W 3**	180,000	❻		
Life membership	**W 4**	4,000	❸		
Entrance fees		17,000	❶		
Annual sponsorship		33,000	❶		
Profit from catering		2,190	❷	270,885	
Less Expenditure					
Sundry expenses (185,600 – 2,400)		183,200	❸		
Loan interest		3,600	❷		
Depreciation – Equipment		14,620	❷		
Depreciation – Clubhouse & Courts		14,800	❷		
Coaching Lessons		4,650	❶	220,870	
Surplus of income over expenditure for year				50,015	❸

(c) **20**

Balance Sheet as at 31/12/2003

	Cost		Dep to date		NBV	
Fixed Assets	€		€		€	
Clubhouse & Courts	740,000	❶	14,800	❶	725,200	
Equipment	73,100	❷	14,620	❶	58,480	
	813,100		29,420		783,680	
Investments						
6% Government investments			40,000	❶		
Building Society			70,000	❶	110,000	
					893,680	
Current Assets						
Bar stock			4,300	❶		
Bar debtors			110	❶		
Investment income due			1,100	❸		
Bank			5,190	❶		
			10,700			
Less Creditors: amounts falling due within 1 year						
Subscriptions prepaid	2,400	❶				
Bar creditors	2,770	❶	5,170			
Working Capital					5,530	
Total Net Assets					899,210	
Financed by						
Creditors: amounts falling due after more than 1 year						
Life membership					44,000	❷
Levy reserve Fund					120,000	❷
Accumulated fund						
Balance at 1 January 2003			685,195	❶		
Add excess of income for year			50,015		735,210	
Capital employed					899,210	

(d) **15**

A reduction in subscriptions of 20% for 2004 would involve a reduction in club income of €36,000. ❻

Although the club is financially sound as it has €5,190 in the bank, €70,000 in the building society, investments worth €40,000 and has paid off a loan of €30,000, these funds are set aside for future capital expenditure. ❸

The club's surplus of income for the year 2003 of €50,015 would seem to indicate that the club is capable of bearing a reduction of 20%. However, almost all of this surplus is provided by entrance fees of €17,000 and sponsorship of €33,000 and this income cannot be guaranteed in future years. ❸

It can be argued that a reduction in membership fees could attract more members and thus bring in entrance fees as well as increase bar profit. However, it would *not* be prudent to reduce subscription fees at present and instead it would be advisable to retain the present level of fees and use these fees to provide improved facilities for the members and thus attract more members. ❸

Workings

1 Bar Profit – Bar Trading Account for year ended 31/12/2003

	€	€
Sales (112,660 – 155 + 110)		112,615
Less Cost of goods sold		
Stock at 1 January 2003	3,800	
Add purchases (80,500 + 2,770 – 2,450)	80,820	
Less Stock 31 December 2003	(4,300)	80,320
Bar profit		32,295

2 Investment Income

	€	
Income Received	1,450	
Less Income due 1/1/2003	(150)	
Add Income due 31/12/2003	1,100	
Income and expenditure account		2,400

3 Subscriptions

	€	
Subscriptions received	254,200	
Add subscriptions prepaid at 1/1/2003	1,800	
Less subscriptions prepaid at 31/12/2003	(2,400)	
Less Levy for 2003	(60,000)	
Less Levy for 2002	(1,600)	
Less 2 life memberships	(12,000)	
Income and Expenditure Account		180,000

4 Life Membership 1/1/2003

Life Membership 1/1/2003	36,000	
Add membership received	12,000	
Less amount transferred to I & E account	(4,000)	
Balance 31/12/2003		44,000

5 Profit on Catering – catering receipts

Profit on Catering – catering receipts	6,650	
Catering costs	4,460	
Income and expenditure account		2,190

Question 7

55

(a)

Journal Entries

		Dr	Cr
		€	€
(i)	Fixtures & Fittings	1,650 ❸	
	Purchases	16,500 ❸	
	Creditors/Dolan		23,000 ❸
	Suspense	4,850 ❸	
	Being correction of incorrect recording of the purchase of furniture on credit		
(ii)	Debtor account	800 ❷	
	Bank account		750 ❷
	Discount Allowed disallowed		50 ❸
	Bad Debts account	800 ❸	
	Debtor		800 ❷
	Being recording of dishonouring a cheque and recording of a bad debt		
(iii)	Fixtures and Fittings	34 ❸	
	Purchases		40 ❸
	Suspense	6 ❸	
	Sales Returns	340 ❷	
	Debtors		340 ❷
	Being lockers returned by a customer entered incorrectly in the books		
(iv)	Drawings	1,600 ❸	
	Discount Allowed	100 ❸	
	Debtors		1,700 ❸
	Being recording of an offset of a private debt owed by Craddock against a debt owed by a customer to the firm		
(v)	Creditors	8,320 ❸	
	Suspense		8,600 ❸
	Purchases Returns	280 ❸	
	Being correction of incorrect recording of a credit note and recording of a charge for returns		

Penalty of 5 × 1 mark for each narrative omitted

10

(b)

Suspense Account

		€			€
Purchases	(i)	4,850 ❸			
Purchases	(ii)	6 ❸			
*Original difference		3,744 ❶	Creditors	(v)	8,600 ❸
		8,600			8,600

*Originally included in stock. The stock figure is now €88,600 – €3,744 = €84,856

(c)

15

Statement of Correct Net Profit

		€	€
Original net profit as per books			63,300 ❶
Add	Discount disallowed		50 ❷
	Purchases		40 ❷
			63,390
Less	Purchases	16,500 ❶	
	Bad debts	800 ❶	
	Sales Returns	340 ❶	
	Discount allowed	100 ❶	
	Purchases returns	280 ❷	18,020
Correct Net Profit			45,370 ❹

(d)

20

Balance Sheet as at 31/12/2003

		€	€	€
Fixed Assets				
Premises				650,000 ❶
Fixtures & Fittings	(72,000 + 1,650 + 34)			73,684 ❸
				723,684
Current Assets				
Stock	(88,600 – 3,744)		84,856 ❷	
Debtors	(33,300 – 1,700 – 340)		31,260 ❸	
Cash			400 ❶	
			116,516	
Less Creditors: amounts falling due within 1 year				
Creditors	(52,000 – 8,320 + 23,000)	66,680 ❸		
Bank	(27,000 + 750)	27,750 ❷	94,430	22,086
				745,770 ❶
Financed by				
Capital			730,000 ❶	
+ Net Profit			45,370	
			775,370	
– Drawings	(28,000 + 1,600)		29,600 ❷	745,770
				745,770 ❶

Question 8

68

		€	€ (per unit)
Sales: (60,000 @ €16)		960,000	16.00
Less Variable costs:			
Direct materials	331,000		
Direct labour	158,300		
Factory overheads (30%)	24,300		
Sales Commission (70c × 60,000)	42,000		
Total variable costs		555,600	9.26
Contribution		404,400	**6.74**
Less Fixed Costs:			
Factory overheads (70%)	56,700		
Administration expenses	113,400		
Selling expenses (excluding commission)	36,000	206,100	
Net Profit		198,300	

(a) **Break-even point** $= \frac{\text{Fixed Costs}}{\text{CPU}} = \frac{€206{,}100}{€6.74}$ = **30,579 units** ⓮

Margin of safety = Budgeted sales less break-even point

= 60,000 – 30,579 = **29,421 units** ❻

(b) **Sales in units required to provide increase of 15% in net profit**

	€
Net Profit 2003	198,300
Increase in Net profit 2003 (+ 15%)	29,745
Net profit required 2004	228,045

$\frac{\text{Fixed Costs + Profit target}}{\text{CPU}} = \frac{€206{,}100 + 228{,}045}{€6.74}$ = **64,414 units** ⓬

(c) Selling price for 2004

Profit if selling price dropped to €14 in 2004		**€**
Sales	(75,000 × €14.00)	1,050,000
Less Variable costs	(75,000 × €9.26)	694,500
Contribution		355,500
Less Fixed Costs	(206,100 + 14,000)	220,100
Profit		135,400 ⓬

(d)

2003 Fixed costs	206,100
2003 Fixed costs + 10%	20,610
2004 Fixed costs	226,710

Contribution required for 2004 = Fixed costs + Profit
= 226,710 + 198,300 = €425,010

Contribution per unit 2004 $= \frac{\text{Total contribution}}{\text{Budgeted sales (in units)}} = \frac{€425,010}{60,000} = €7.0835$

Variable costs per unit = €9.2600

Selling price = **€16.3435** ⓬

(e) $\frac{\text{Fixed Costs}}{\text{Contribution} - 10\% \text{ of S.P.}}$ $\frac{€206,100}{€7.74 - 1.70}$ **34,123 units** ⓬

(f) 2 × 6 marks **12**

Variable costs are assumed to be completely variable at all levels of output. However, variable costs may decrease due to economy of scale or may increase because of increased costs.

It is assumed that in marginal costing fixed costs remain the same although most fixed costs are step-fixed and are only fixed within a relevant range.

It is assumed that all mixed costs are easily separated into fixed or variable. The High Lo method can be used for this purpose but it is not always possible to do this.

It is assumed that the selling price per unit is constant and does not allow for discounts.

Production in a period usually equals sales. Fixed costs are charged in total to a period and are not carried forward to next period.

Question 9

60

(a)

Cash Forecast July/December

	July	Aug	Sept	Oct	Nov	Dec
Receipts	€	€	€	€	€	€
Cash sales receipts	149,625 ❶	167,580 ❶	175,560 ❶	179,550 ❶	187,530 ❶	191,520 ❶
Credit sales receipts 1 month		183,750 ❶	205,800 ❶	215,600 ❶	220,500 ❶	230,300 ❶
Credit sales receipts 2 months			183,750 ❶	205,800 ❶	215,600 ❶	220,500 ❶
	149,625	351,330	565,110	600,950	623,630	642,320
Payments						
Equipment	48,000 ❷					
Wages/Labour	45,000 ❶	45,000 ❶	45,000 ❶	45,000 ❶	45,000 ❶	45,000 ❶
Variable overheads	75,000 ❶	84,000 ❶	88,000 ❶	90,000 ❶	94,000 ❶	96,000 ❶
Fixed overheads	51,200 ❷	51,200 ❶	51,200 ❶	51,200 ❶	51,200 ❶	51,200 ❶
Interest	417 ❷	417 ❶	417 ❶	417 ❶	417 ❶	417 ❶
Purchases – materials		147,000 ❶	314,640 ❶	340,480 ❶	352,400 ❶	364,240 ❶
	219,617	327,617	499,257	527,097	543,017	556,857
Net monthly Cash Flow	(69,992) ❶	23,713 ❶	65,853 ❶	73,853 ❶	80,613 ❶	85,463 ❶
Bank loan – Financing	50,000 ❶					
Opening balance		(19,992) ❶	3,721	69,574	143,427	224,040 ❶
Closing balance	(19,992)	3,721	69,574	143,427	224,040	309,503 ❸

Workings – Equipment Cost €48,000. Depreciation €9,600 p.a. (€800 per month) is a non cash item.

20

(b)

Budgeted Profit and Loss Account

	€	€
Sales: (52,700 @ €70)		3,689,000 ❷
Less Cost of sales – Material (52,700 × €40)	2,108,000 ❷	
– Labour	270,000 ❷	
– Variable overheads	527,000 ❷	
Fixed overheads (€51,200 × 6)	307,200 ❷	3,212,200
Gross profit		476,800
Depreciation Equipment	4,800 ❷	
Discount Allowed (€3,689,000 × 30% × 5%)	55,335 ❷	60,135
		416,665
Add Discount Received (€1,724,000 × 50% × 2%)		17,240 ❷
		433,905
Less Interest		2,500 ❷
Profit		431,405 ❷

LEAVING CERTIFICATE EXAMINATION, 2003

ACCOUNTING – HIGHER LEVEL

(400 marks)

THURSDAY, 12 JUNE 2003 – MORNING 9.30 a.m. to 12.30 p.m.

This paper is divided into 3 Sections:

Section 1: Financial Accounting (120 marks).

This section has 4 questions (Numbers 1–4). The first question carries 120 marks and the remaining three questions carry 60 marks each.
Candidates should answer either **QUESTION 1 only** OR else attempt any **TWO** of the remaining three questions in this section.

Section 2: Financial Accounting (200 marks).

This section has three questions (Numbers 5–7). Each question carries 100 marks.
Candidates should answer any **TWO** questions.

Section 3: Management Accounting (80 marks).

This section has two questions (Numbers 8 and 9). Each question carries 80 marks.
Candidates should answer **ONE** of these questions.

Calculators

Calculators may be used in answering the questions on this paper: however, it is very important that workings are shown in the answer book(s) so that full credit can be given for correct work.

SECTION 1 (120 marks)

Answer **Question 1** OR any **TWO** other questions

---

1. Sole Trader – Final Accounts

The following trial balance was extracted from the books of M. O'Brien on 31/12/2002.

	€	€
9% Investments 1/6/2002	200,000	
Buildings (cost €980,000)	933,000	
Delivery vans (cost €150,000)	80,500	
5% Fixed Mortgage (including increase of €200,000 5% mortgage received on 1/4/2002)		500,000
Patents (incorporating 3 months investment income)	55,500	
Debtors and Creditors	77,600	86,500
Purchases and Sales	668,000	982,000
Stocks 1/1/2002	67,700	
Commission	24,000	
Provision for Bad Debts		3,800
Salaries and General Expenses	194,100	
Discount (net)		4,600
Rent		15,000
Mortgage Interest paid for first 3 months	4,000	
Insurance (incorporating suspense)	8,700	
VAT		5,500
PRSI		2,300
Bank		70,900
Drawings	37,500	
Capital		680,000
	2,350,600	2,350,600

The following information and instructions are to be taken into account:

(i) Stock at 31/12/2002 at cost was €74,500. This figure includes damaged stock which cost €6,600 but which now has a net realisable value of €1,900.

(ii) Provide for depreciation on vans at the annual rate of 15% of cost from the date of purchase to the date of sale.
NOTE: On 31/3/2002 a delivery van which had cost €42,000 on 31/5/1999 was traded against a new van which cost €48,000. An allowance of €20,000 was made on the old van. The cheque for the net amount of this transaction was entered in the bank account but was incorrectly treated as a purchase of trading stock. These were the only entries made in the books in respect of this transaction.

(iii) Patents, which incorporate 3 months investment income, are to be written off over a 5 year period commencing in 2002.

(iv) The suspense figure arises as a result of the posting of an incorrect figure for mortgage interest to the mortgage interest account and discount received €700 entered only in the creditors account. The correct interest was entered in the bank account.

(v) Provision to be made for mortgage interest due.

(vi) A new warehouse was purchased during the year for €240,000 plus VAT 12.5%. The amount paid to the vendor was entered in the Buildings account. No entry was made in the VAT account.

(vii) Provide for depreciation on buildings at the rate of 2% *of cost* per annum. It was decided to re-value the buildings at €1,100,000 on 31/12/2002.

(viii) Provision for bad debts to be adjusted to 4% of debtors.

You are required to prepare a:

(a) Trading and profit and loss account for the year ended 31/12/2002. (75)

(b) Balance sheet as at 31/12/2002. (45)

(120 marks)

2. Published accounts

Oatfield Plc has an Authorised Capital of €900,000 divided into 700,000 Ordinary Shares at €l each and 200,000 8% Preference Shares at €l each. The following Trial Balance was extracted from its books on 31/12/2002.

	€	€
Patent	56,000	
9% Investments 1/1/2002	120,000	
Land and buildings (re-valued on 1/7/2002)	880,000	
Revaluation reserve		260,000
Delivery vans at cost	145,000	
Delivery vans — accumulated depreciation on 1/1/2002		68,000
Debtors and Creditors	187,000	98,000
Purchases and Sales	696,000	1,105,000
Stocks 1/1/2002	75,000	
Directors' Fees	84,000	
Salaries and General Expenses	177,000	
Discount		6,160
Advertising	21,000	
Investment Income		8,100
Profit on sale of Land		85,000
Rent	32,000	
Interim dividends for first 6 months	27,000	
Profit and Loss Balance 1/1/2002		73,700

8% Debentures (2008/2009) including €120,000 8% Debentures issued on 1/8/2002		270,000
Bank		17,740
VAT		8,300
Issued Capital		
350,000 Ordinary Shares at €1 each		350,000
150,000 8% Preference Shares		150,000
	2,500,000	2,500,000

The following information is also relevant:

(i) Stock on 31/12/2002 was valued on a first in first out basis at €77,000.

(ii) The patent was acquired on 1/1/1999 for €80,000. It is being amortised over 10 years in equal instalments. The amortisation should be included in cost of sales.

(iii) On 1/7/2002 the ordinary shareholders received an interim dividend of €21,000 and the preference shareholders received €6,000. The directors propose the payment of the preference dividend due and a final dividend on ordinary shares bringing the total ordinary dividend up to 16c per share for the year.

(iv) On 1/7/2002 land, which had cost €90,000, was sold for €175,000. On this date the remaining land and buildings were re-valued at €880,000. Included in this revaluation is land now valued at €180,000 but which originally cost €70,000. The re-valued buildings had cost €550,000.

(v) Depreciation is to be provided as follows:
Delivery vans at the rate of 20% of cost Buildings at the rate of 2% of cost per annum until date of revaluation and thereafter at 2% per annum of revalued figure.

(vi) Provide for debenture interest due, investment income due, auditors fees €7,700 and taxation €33,000.

You are required to:

(a) Prepare the published profit and loss account for the year ended 31/12/2002 in accordance with the Companies Acts and financial reporting standards showing the following notes:

1. Accounting policy note for stock and depreciation
2. Dividends
3. Interest payable
4. Operating profit
5. Profit on sale of property (50)

(b) Name the agencies that regulate the production, content and presentation of company financial statements. (10)

(60 marks)

3. Debtors Control Account

The Debtors Ledger Control Account of T. O'Dowd showed the following balances — €33,444dr and €633cr on 31/12/2002. These figures did not agree with the Schedule (List) of Debtors Balances extracted on the same date. An examination of the books revealed the following:

(i) A cheque for €850, received from a customer in full settlement of a debt of €880, had been entered correctly in the books. However, this cheque was dishonoured but no entry had been made in the books relating to the cancelled cheque.

(ii) Cash sales €1,800 and credit sales €800 had both been entered by O'Dowd on the credit of a customer's account.

(iii) O'Dowd had sent an invoice to a customer for €1,680. This had been entered in the appropriate day book as €1,860. However, when posting from this book to the ledger no entry had been made in the customer account.

(iv) A credit note was sent to a customer for €566. The only entry made in the books was €56 debited to the customer's account.

(v) O'Dowd had charged a customer interest amounting to €82 on an overdue account. The only entry in the books for this interest had been €28 credited to the customer's account. After a protest this interest was reduced to €20 but this reduction had not been reflected in the accounts.

(vi) O'Dowd had accepted sales returns €400 from a customer and entered this correctly in the books. However, a credit note was sent out by the secretary showing a restocking charge of 10% of sales price. The secretary made the necessary adjustment only in the customer's account. Later this charge was reduced to 6% but this reduction was not reflected in the accounts.

You are required to show the following:

(a) Adjusted Debtors' Ledger Control Account. (35)

(b) Adjusted Schedule of Debtors' showing the original balance. (25)

(60 marks)

4. Revaluation of Fixed Assets

On 1 January 1998 O'Flynn Ltd owned property which cost €630,000, consisting of Land €210,000 and Buildings €420,000. The company depreciates its assets at the rate of 2% using the straight line method. It is the company's policy to apply a full year's depreciation in the year of acquisition and nil depreciation in the year of disposal. This property had been purchased ten years earlier and depreciation had been charged against profits in each of these ten years (Land is not depreciated).

The following details were taken from the firm's books:

Jan 1 1998 Revalued property at €750,000. Of this revaluation €250,000 was attributable to land.

Jan 1 1999 Sold for €320,000 land which cost €210,000 but was since revalued on 1/1/1998.

Jan 1 2000 Purchased buildings for €340,000. During the year 2000, €80,000 was paid to a building contractor for an extension to these recently purchased buildings. The company's own employees also worked on the extension and they were paid wages amounting to €30,000 by O'Flynn Ltd for this work.

Jan 1 2001 Revalued buildings owned at €1,045,000 (a 10% increase in respect of each building).

Jan 1 2002 Sold for €590,000 the buildings owned on 1/1/1998. The remaining buildings were revalued at €620,000.

You are required to:

Prepare the relevant ledger accounts in respect of the above transactions for the five years to 31 December 2002. (**Bank Account and Profit and Loss Account <u>not</u> required**)

(60 marks)

SECTION 2 (200 marks)

Answer **ANY TWO** questions

---

5. Interpretation of Accounts

The following figures have been extracted from the final accounts of O'Gara Plc, a manufacturer in the healthcare industry, for the year ended 31 December 2002.

Trading and Profit and Loss account for year ended 31/12/2002

	€
Sales	980,000
Costs of goods sold	(620,000)
Total operating expenses for year	(207,000)
Interest for year	(10,000)
Net profit for year	143,000
Proposed dividends	(68,000)
Retained profit for year	75,000

Ratios and figures for year ended 31/12/2001

Earnings per ordinary share	18c
Dividend per ordinary share	6.5c
Quick ratio	0.75 to 1
Market price of ordinary share	€1.90
Return on capital employed	14%
Return on equity funds	7.6%
Interest cover	9 times
Gearing	35%

Balance Sheet as at 31/12/2002

Intangible Assets	160,000	
Tangible assets	790,000	950,000
Current assets (including stock €66,000, debtors €74,000)		160,000
Trade creditors		(73,000)
Dividends		(68,000)
		969,000
10% Debentures 2008/2009		100,000
Issued capital		
650,000 Ordinary shares @ €1 each		650,000
100,000 13% Preference shares @ €l each		100,000
Profit and loss balance		119,000
		969,000

You are required to:

(a) Calculate the following for 2002:

(i) Cash sales if the average period of credit to debtors is 1 month.

(ii) Earnings per share.

(iii) The market price of one ordinary share if the Price Earnings ratio is 11.

(iv) The ordinary dividend cover.

(v) The dividend yield. (50)

(b) A friend of yours has been given the opportunity to buy ordinary shares in O'Gara Plc but before doing so asks your opinion. What advice would you give? Use ratios, percentages and other information from the above to support your conclusions.

(50)

(100 marks)

6. Service Company Accounts

Included in the assets and liabilities of the Slimline Health Centre Ltd on 1/1/2002 were the following:

Buildings and Grounds at cost €520,000; Equipment at cost €90,000; Furniture at cost €25,000; Stock of health food for sale €1,500; Heating oil €660; Contract cleaning prepaid €300; Creditors for supplies to health centre €1,450; Clients' Fees paid in Advance €5,500, Investments €80,000; Authorised Capital, €450,000; Issued Capital €320,000.

All fixed assets have 3 years accumulated depreciation on 1/1/2002.

Receipts and Payments Account of Slimline Health Centre Ltd for the year ended 31/12/2002

Receipts	€	**Payments**	€
Current a/c balance	7,560	Wages and salaries	88,240
Client's fees	262,600	Insurance	6,300
Interest	2,160	Light and heat	2,900
Shop receipts	67,000	Purchases – shop	41,300
Balance	9,500	Purchases – supplies	38,600
		Laundry	4,100
		New extension 1/1/2002	80,000
		Contract Cleaning	2,700
		Telephone and postage	1,880
		Equipment	16,000
		Repayment of €60,000 loan on 1/6/2002 with **17 months** interest	66,800
	€348,820		€348,820

You are given the following additional information and instructions:

1. Closing stock at 31/12/2002: Shop €1,800; Heating Oil €360; Electricity due 31/12/2002 €290.
2. Cleaning is done by contract payable monthly in advance and includes a payment of €400 for January 2003.
3. Clients' fees include fees for 2003 of €4,000.
4. Clients' fees in arrears at 31/12/2002 €650.
5. Wages and salaries include €16,000 per annum paid to the receptionist who also runs the shop. It is estimated that 60% of this salary and €220 of the light and heat, €600 of the insurance and €360 of the telephone is attributable to the shop.
6. Slimline Health Centre Ltd decided to revalue buildings and grounds at €700,000 on 31/12/2002.
7. Depreciation to be provided as follows:
   Buildings – 2% of cost for a full year.
   Equipment – 20% of cost per annum.
   Furniture – 20% of cost per annum.
8. Creditors for supplies to health centre at 31/12/2002 €1,600.

You are required to:

(a) Calculate the company's reserves on 1/1/2002. (20)

(b) Calculate the Profit/loss from the health shop for the year ended 31/12/2002. (12)

(c) Prepare a Profit and Loss Account for the year ended 31/12/2002. (36)

(d) Prepare a Balance Sheet on 31/12/2002. (32)

(100 marks)

7. Incomplete records

J. O'Higgins lodged €350,000 to a business bank account on 1/1/2002 and on the same day purchased a business for €320,000, including the following assets and liabilities: buildings €290,000, stock €16,700, three months rates prepaid €2,400, debtors €32,500, wages due €3,600 and trade creditors €58,000.

O'Higgins did not keep a full set of books during 2002 but estimates that the gross profit was 40% of sales and he was able to supply the following additional information on 31/12/2002:

(i) Each week O'Higgins took from stock goods to the value of €100 and cash €150 for household expenses.

(ii) On 1/10/2002 O'Higgins borrowed €300,000, part of which was used to purchase an adjoining premises costing €250,000. It was agreed that O'Higgins would pay interest on the last day of the month at the rate of 6% per annum. The capital sum was to be repaid in one lump sum in the year 2010 and, to provide for this, the bank was instructed to transfer €2,500 on the last day of every month from O'Higgins's business account into an investment fund.

(iii) During the year, O'Higgins lodged dividends €2,500 to the business bank and made the following payments: light and heat €7,200, interest €3,000, wages and general expenses €98,000, equipment €16,000, rates for twelve months €10,800 and college fees €4,500.

(iv) O'Higgins estimated that 25% of the following: equipment, light and heat ***used*** and interest ***payable*** should be attributed to the private section of the premises. O'Higgins further estimates that 70% of college fees should be attributed to a family member and the remainder to an employee.

(v) Included in the assets and liabilities of the firm on 31/12/2002 were stock €17,200, debtors €34,300, trade creditors €29,900, cash at bank €68,462, electricity due €560 and €75 interest earned by the investment fund to date.

You are required to prepare, with workings, a:

(a) Statement/Balance Sheet showing O'Higgins's profit or loss for the year ended 31/12/2002. (50)

(b) Trading, Profit and Loss Account, in as much detail as possible, for the year ended 31/12/2002. (40)

(c) Summary of the advice you would give to O'Higgins in relation to the information given above. (10)

(100 marks)

SECTION 3 (80 marks)

Answer **ONE** question

Question 8 – Costing

(a) Valuation of Closing Stock

The following information relates to the purchases and sales (exclusive of VAT) of O'Leary Ltd for the year 2002:

Period	Details	Quantity and Price
01/01/02 to 31/03/02	Purchases on credit	4,200 @ €7 each
	Credit sales	1,300 @ €12 each
	Cash sales	1,200 @ €11 each
01/04/02 to 30/06/02	Purchases on credit	3,200 @ €7 each
	Credit sales	1,350 @ €12 each
	Cash sales	1,500 @ €12 each
01/07/02 to 30/09/02	Purchases on credit	2,700 @ €8 each
	Credit sales	1,400 @ €13 each
	Cash sales	1,200 @ €11 each
01/10/02 to 31/12/02	Purchases on credit	2,300 @ €9 each
	Credit sales	1,600 @ €13 each
	Cash sales	900 @ €13 each

On 1/1/2002 there was an opening stock of 4,400 units @ €7 each.

You are required to:

(i) Calculate the value of the closing stock, using the first in first out (FIFO) method.

(ii) Prepare a trading account for the year ended 31/12/2002.

(b) Product Costing

O'Mahony Ltd is a small company with three departments. The following are the company's budgeted costs for the coming year.

Department	Variable Costs	Fixed Costs	Wage Rate per hour
X	€18 per hour	€8.50 per hour	€11
Y	€16 per hour	€7.50 per hour	€12
Z	€20 per hour	€4.00 per hour	€10

General administration overhead absorption rate per hour is budgeted to be €4.50.

The following are the specifications for a quotation for Job No. 999:
Material costs €6,450.
Labour hours required in each department are:

Department	**Hours**
X	90
Y	180
Z	50

You are required to:

(i) Calculate the selling price of Job No. 999 if the profit is set at 25% of selling price.

(ii) State two reasons for product costing and explain each.

(80 marks)

9. Flexible Budgeting

O'Reilly manufactures a component for the electronics industry. The following flexible budgets have already been prepared for 55%,70% and 85% of the plant's capacity:

Output levels	**55%**	**70%**	**85%**
Units	11,000	14,000	17,000
Costs	**€**	**€**	**€**
Direct materials	143,000	182,000	221,000
Direct wages	99,000	126,000	153,000
Production overheads	74,000	92,000	110,000
Other overhead costs	36,000	45,000	54,000
Administration expenses	29,000	29,000	29,000
	381,000	474,000	567,000

Profit is budgeted to be 22% of sales.

You are required to:

(a) (i) Classify the above costs into fixed, variable and mixed costs.

(ii) Separate production overheads into fixed and variable elements.

(iii) Separate other overhead costs into fixed and variable elements.

(iv) Prepare a flexible budget for 96% activity level.

(v) Restate the budget, using marginal costing principles, and show the contribution.

(b) Explain Principal Budget Factor. Why prepare a flexible budget and what does it show?

(80 marks)

Accounting – Higher Level 2003

Solutions

Question 1

75

(a)

Trading, Profit and Loss Account the year ended 31/12/2002

		€	€	€
Sales				982,000 ❷
Less Cost of sales				
Stock 1/1/2002			67,700 ❷	
Add Purchases	W 1		640,000 ❻	
			707,700	
Less Stock 31/12/2002	W 2		(69,800) ❻	(637,900)
Gross profit				344,100
Less Expenses				
Administration				
Salaries and general expenses		194,100 ❷		
Patents written off	W 3	12,000 ❻		
Insurance	W 4	9,650 ❽		
Depreciation – buildings	W 5	19,000 ❸	234,750	
Selling and Distribution				
Loss on sale of delivery van	W 7	4,150 ❻		
Commission		24,000 ❷		
Depreciation – delivery vans	W 6	23,175 ❺	51,325	(286,075)
				58,025
Add Operating income				
Reduction in provision for bad debts	W 8			696 ❹
Rent				15,000 ❷
Discount	W 9			5,300 ❺
Operating profit				79,021
Investment income				10,500 ❸
				89,521
Mortgage interest	W 10			(22,500) ❻
Net profit for year				**67,021** ❼

(b) **45**

Balance Sheet as at 31 December 2002

		Cost	Accumulated Depreciation	Net	Total
Intangible Fixed Assets		€	€	€	€
Patents (€60,000 – €12,000)					48,400 ❹
Tangible Fixed Assets					
Buildings	**W 11**	1,100,000 ❷		1,100,000	
Delivery vans		156,000 ❷	74,825 ❸	81,175	
		1,256,000	74,825	1,181,175	1,181,175
Financial Assets					
Investments					200,000 ❷
					1,429,175
Current assets					
Stock				69,800 ❷	
VAT	**W 12**			24,500 ❺	
Investment income due				6,000 ❸	
Debtors			77,600 ❷		
Less provision			3,104 ❶	74,496	
				174,796	
Creditors: amounts falling due within one year					
Creditors			86,500 ❷		
Mortgage interest due			18,750 ❸		
PRSI			2,300 ❷		
Bank			70,900 ❷	(178,450)	(3,654)
					1,425,521
Financed by					
Creditors: amounts falling due after more than one year					
9% Fixed mortgage					500,000 ❷
Capital and reserves					
Capital 1/1/2002				680,000 ❶	
Add Net profit				67,021 ❶	
				747,021	
Less Drawings				37,500 ❷	
				709,521	
Revaluation reserve	**W 13**			216,000 ❹	925,521
Capital employed					1,425,521

Question 1 – *Workings*

1.	**Purchases**	668,000	
	Less Payment for van	(28,000)	640,000
2.	**Closing stock**	74,500	
	Less valueless stock	(4,700)	69,800
3.	**Patents**		
	(€55,500 + €4,500) ÷ 5		12,000
4.	**Insurance**	8,700	
	Add Mortgage interest	250	
	Add Discount received	700	9,650
5.	**Depreciation – buildings**		
	2% of €950,000		19,000
6.	**Depreciation – delivery vans**		
	(€22,500 + €675) (€5,625 + €17,550) (€16,200 + €1,575 + €5,400)		23,175
7.	**Loss on sale of van**		
	(€42,000 – €17,850 – €20,000)		4,150 loss
	Provision for Depreciation – vans		
	(€69,500 – €17,850 + €23,175)		74,825
8.	**Provision for bad debts**		
	(€3,800 – €3,104)		696cr
9.	**Discount**	4,600	
	Add Unrecorded Discount	700	5,300
10.	**Mortgage interest**	4,000	
	Less Suspense	(250)	
	Add Interest due	18,750	22,500
11.	**Buildings**	980,00	
	Less VAT	(30,000)	
	Add Revaluation	150,000	1,100,000
12.	**VAT account**	5,500	
	Less VAT on buildings	(30,000)	24,500
13.	**Revaluation reserve**		
	Land and buildings	150,000	
	Provision for depreciation (47,000 + 19,000)	66,000	216,000

Question 2 – Published Accounts

(a) **38**

Profit and Loss Account of North Plc for the year ended 31/12/2002

		Notes		€
Turnover				1,105,000 ❶
Cost of Sales (75,000 + 696,000 – 77,000 + 8000)		1		702,000 ❼
Gross profit				403,000
Distribution costs	W 1		50,000 ❷	
Administrative expenses	W 2		313,200 ❼	363,200
				39,800
Other operating income				
Discount				6,160 ❶
Operating profit		2		45,960
Profit on sale of land				85,000 ❷
Investment income				10,800 ❸
				141,760
Interest payable		3		16,000 ❸
Profit on ordinary activities before taxation ❶				125,760
Taxation				33,000 ❶
Profit after taxation				92,760
Dividends paid		4	27,000 ❷	
Dividends proposed		4	41,000 ❸	68,000
Profit retained for year				24,760
Profit brought forward at 1/1/2002				73,700 ❶
Profit carried forward at 31/12/2002				98,460 ❹

Notes to the Accounts

1. **Accounting policy notes** ❸
   Tangible Fixed Assets
   Depreciation is calculated in order to write off the value or cost of tangible fixed assets over their estimated useful economic life, as follows:

Buildings –	2% per annum – straight line basis.
Delivery vans –	20% of cost
Stocks –	Stocks are valued on a First in first out basis at the lower of cost and net realisable value.

2. **Dividends** ❹

Ordinary dividends		
Interim paid 6.0c per share	21,000	
Final proposed 10.0c per share	35,000	56,000
Preference dividends		
Interim paid 4.0c per share	6,000	
Final proposed 4.0c per share	6,000	12,000

3. **Interest payable:** ❶
   Interest payable on debentures repayable during years 2008/2009 — 16,000

4. **Operating profit** ❸
   The operating profit is arrived at after charging:

Depreciation on tangible fixed assets	41,500
Patent amortised	8,000
Directors remuneration	84,000
Auditors Fees	7,700

5. **Profit on sale of property** ❶
   The company sold land for €85,000 greater than it cost. Cost was €90,000.

Workings

1. **Distribution costs**

Advertising	21,000	
Depreciation – delivery vans	29,000	50,000

2. **Administrative expenses**

Directors fees	84,000	
Salaries and general expenses	177,000	
Rent	32,000	
Auditors fees	7,700	
Depreciation – buildings	12,500	313,200

(b) 10

Agencies
The Government – Legislation
The European Union – directives
The Accountancy profession – FRSs and SSAPs
The Stock Exchange – Listing Rules

Question 3 – Control Accounts

(a) 35

Adjusted Debtors Ledger Control Account

		€			€
Balance b/d		33,444 ❶	Balance b/d		633 ❸
Dishonoured cheque	(a)	880 ❻	Sales overstated	(c)	180 ❻
Interest	(e)	20 ❻	Credit note	(d)	566 ❻
Restocking charge	(f)	24 ❻	Balance c/d		33,622
Balance c/d		633 ❶			
		35,001			35,001
Balance b/d		33,622	Balance b/d		633

(b) **25**

Schedule of Debtors Account Balances

				€
Balance as per List of Debtors				27,619❺
Add	Dishonoured cheque	(a)	880❸	
	Sales – cash and credit error	(b)	3,400❺	
	Sales	(c)	1,680❸	
	Interest	(e)	48❷	6,008
				33,627
Deduct	Credit note	(d)	622❷	
	Reduction in restocking charge	(f)	16❸	638
Net balance as per adjusted control account				32,989❷

Question 4 – Revaluation of Fixed Assets

(a) **60**

Land and Buildings Account

		€			€
1/1/98	Balance b/d	630,000❷			
1/1/98	Revaluation Res.	120,000❷	31/12/98	Balance c/d	750,000
		750,000			750,000
1/1/99	Balance b/d	750,000	01/01/99	Disposal	250,000❶
			31/12/99	Balance c/d	500,000
		750,000			750,000
1/1/00	Balance b/d	500,000❶	31/12/00	Balance c/d	950,000
	Bank	340,00❷			
	Bank	80,000❷			
	Wages	30,000❷			
		950,000			950,000
1/1/01	Balance b/d	950,000	31/12/01	Balance c/d	1,045,000
1/1/01	Revaluation Reserve	95,000❷			
		1,045,000			1,045,000
1/1/02	Balance b/d	1,045,000	01/01/02	Disposal	550,000❸
1/1/02	Revaluation Reserve	125,000❸	31/12/02	Balance c/d	620,000
		1,170,000			1,170,000

Provision for Depreciation on Buildings Account

Date	Details	€	Date	Details	€
1/1/98	Revaluation Res	84,000❷	1/1/98	Balance b/d	84,000❹
31/12/98	Balance c/d	10,000	31/12/98	Profit and Loss	10,000❷
		94,000			94,000
31/12/99	Balance c/d	20,000	1/1/99	Balance b/d	10,000
			31/12/99	Profit and Loss	10,000❷
		20,000			20,000
31/12/00	Balance c/d	39,000	1/1/00	Balance b/d	20,000
			31/12/00	Profit and Loss	19,000❷
		39,000			39,000
1/1/01	Revaluation Res	39,000❷	1/1/00	Balance c/d	39,000
31/12/01	Balance c/d	20,900	31/12/01	Profit and Loss	20,900❷
		59,900			59,900
1/1/02	Disposal	11,000❷	1/1/02	Balance b/d	20,900
1/1/02	Revaluation Res.	9,900❸	31/12/02	Profit and Loss	12,400❷
31/12/02	Balance c/d	12,400			
		33,300			33,300
			1/1/03	Balance b/d	12,400

Disposal of Land Account

Date	Details	€	Date	Details	€
1/1/99	Buildings	250,000❶	1/1/99	Bank	320,000❶
31/12/99	P & L (Profit)	70,000❶			
		320,000			320,000

Disposal of Buildings Account

Date	Details	€	Date	Details	€
1/1/02	Buildings	550,000❶	1/1/02	Depreciation	11,000❶
31/12/02	P & L (Profit)	51,000❶	1/1/02	Bank	590,000❶
		601,000			601,000

Revaluation Reserve Account

Date	Details	€	Date	Details	€
1/1/98	Revenue reserve	40,000❶	1/1/98	Land and Buildings	120,000❶
1/1/02	Revenue reserve	244,000❶		Provision for Dep	84,000❶
			1/1/01	Land and Buildings	95,000❶
				Provision for Dep	39,000❶
			1/1/02	Land and Buildings	125,000❶
				Provision for Dep	9,900❶

Revenue Reserve Account

		€
1/1/98	Revenue reserve	40,000 ❶
1/1/02	Revenue reserve	244,000 ❶

Question 5 – Interpretation of Accounts

50

(a)

Cash sales

$$\frac{\text{Debtors} \times 12}{\text{Credit sales}} = 1 \quad \text{Credit sales} = \frac{74{,}000 \times 12}{1}$$

Credit sales = 888,000

Cash sales = 980,000 – 888,000 = **€92,000** ⑫

Earnings per share

$$\frac{\text{Net profit} - \text{Pref Div} \times 100}{\text{Number of ordinary shares}} = \frac{130{,}000 \times 100}{650{,}000} = \mathbf{20c}$$ ⑩

Market Price

$$\frac{\text{Market price}}{\text{Earnings per share}} = 11$$

$$\frac{x}{20} = 11 = \mathbf{220c}$$ ❽

Dividend cover

$$\frac{\text{Net profit after Pref Div}}{\text{Ordinary dividend}} = \frac{130{,}000}{55{,}000} = \mathbf{2.4\ times}$$ ⑩

Dividend Yield

$$\frac{\text{Dividend per share} \times 100}{\text{Market price}} = \frac{8.46p \times 100}{220p} = \mathbf{3.85\%}$$ ⑩

50

(b)

I would advise my friend to buy shares in O'Gara Plc Ltd for the following reasons:

Gearing ⑩
Gearing is 20.6% or 0.26 to 1. The company is low geared at 20.6% and interest cover is 15.3 times. Therefore there is little risk from outside investors. Last year's gearing and interest cover were 35% and 9 times respectively. These figures indicate improved situations and that the company is less at risk and is better able to pay interest in 2002 than in 2001. The prospects of being able to pay dividends are good.

Dividends ⑩
Dividend per share is 8.46c. The dividend per share has increased from 6.5c since 200l. The company's dividend cover is 2.4 times and dividend yield is 3.85%. The dividend policy is such that a shareholder can expect a decent amount of profits will be paid out each year and at the same time the long-term prospects of capital gain are good. The real return to ordinary shareholders would be 9.1% based on available profits.

Profitability ⑩
O'Gara Plc is a profitable firm because its return on capital employed of 15.8% and on equity funds of 6.9% indicate that the firm is earning much more (three times) than the return from risk

free investments of about 4% to 6%. These are big increases from 14% and 7.6% respectively in 2001. The earnings per share has increased by 2c from 18c in 2001 to 20c in 2002.

Liquidity ⑩
O'Gara Plc has a liquidity problem. It would have difficulty paying its immediate debts. This difficulty has worsened since 2001, and the company is less able to pay its immediate debts in 2002 as indicated by the acid test ratio. This ratio has worsened from 0.75 in 2001 to 0.67 in 2002. This ratio indicates that O'Gara Plc has only 67c available to pay each €1 owed immediately. The company had 75c available in 2001.

Reserves ❺
The firm is retaining profits and building up reserves which augers well in the long-term and should bring about an increase in the market price of the share. Reserves have risen by €75,000 to €119,000 since 2001.

Market Price ❺
The share value has gone up by 30c to €2.20 since 2001 and is likely to continue in its upward movement based on current year performance.

Real value of fixed assets/Security: The real value of fixed assets and intangible assets should be questioned. There are no write offs. Although there are intangible assets valued at €160,000 there is little risk to the company as this is only 20% of the tangible fixed assets and this ensures that there is adequate security for the loan.

Sector
The healthcare industry is a growth area and the sector has good prospects.

Price Earnings Ratio
The price earnings ratio is 11. This means that at the present rate of earnings it would take 11 years to earn back the price of a share.

Interest Cover
Interest Cover is 15.3 times and has improved from 9 times in 2001. There should be more profits available to the shareholders.

Question 6 – Final Accounts of a service Firm

(a)

Statement of Capital and Reserves on 1/1/2002

		€	€
Assets			
Buildings and grounds	(520,000 – 31,200)	488,800 ❷	
Equipment	(90,000 – 54,000)	36,000 ❷	
Furniture	(25,000 – 15,000)	10,000 ❷	
Investments		80,000 ❶	
Stock – Health food for resale		1,500 ❶	
Stock-oil		660 ❶	
Contract cleaning prepaid		300 ❶	
Cash at bank		7,560 ❶	624,820
Less Liabilities			
Creditors for supplies		1,450 ❶	
Customers' advance deposits		5,500 ❶	
Loan		60,000 ❷	
Interest on loan	(12 months @ €400 per month)	4,800 ❷	
Issued capital		320,000 ❶	391,750
Reserves			233,070 ❷

12

(b)

Health Shop Profit and Loss Account for year ended 31/12/2002

		€	€
Shop receipts – sales			67,000 ❷
Less Expenses			
Cost of goods sold –	(1,500 + 41,300 – 1,800)	41,000 ❺	
Light and heat		220 ❶	
Insurance		600 ❶	
Telephone		360 ❶	
Wages and Salaries	(60% of 16,000)	9,600 ❷	51,780
Contribution from health shop			15,220

(c) 36

Profit and Loss Account for year ended 31/12/2002

			€	€
Income				
Interest received			2,160 ❶	
Profit on health shop			15,220 ❶	
Customers' fees		W 1	264,750 ❹	282,130
Less Expenses				
Wages and Salaries	(88,240 – 9,600)		78,640 ❷	
Insurance	(6,300 – 600)		5,700 ❶	
Light and heat		W 2	3,270 ❺	
Purchases – supplies		W 3	38,750 ❸	
Loan interest		W 4	2,000 ❸	
Laundry			4,100 ❶	
Postage and telephone			1,520 ❶	
Depreciation – Buildings		W 5	12,000 ❶	
– Equipment			21,200 ❶	
– Furniture			5,000 ❶	
Contract Cleaning		W 6	2,600 ❸	174,780
Net Profit for year				107,350 ❼
Add Reserve 1/1/2002				233,070 ❶
Profit and Loss balance 31/12/2002				340,420

(d) 32

Balance Sheet as at 31/12/2002

		Cost	Depreciation	Net
Fixed Assets		€	€	€
Buildings and Grounds		700,000 ❶		700,000
Equipment	(90,000 + 16,000)	106,000 ❷	75,200 ❷	30,800
Furniture		25,000 ❷	20,000 ❷	5,000
		692,000	107,600	735,800
Investments				80,000 ❷
				815,800
Current Assets				
Closing stock	– shop goods	1,800 ❷		
	– oil	360 ❷		
Cleaning prepaid		400 ❷		
Customers' fees due		650 ❷	3,210	

Less Creditors: amounts falling due within 1 year			
Bank overdraft	9,500 ❷		
Electricity due	290 ❷		
Customers' advance deposits	4,000 ❷		
Creditors for supplies	1,600 ❷	(15,390)	(12,180)
			803,620

Financed by				
Share Capital and reserves		**Authorised**	**Issued**	
Ordinary shares		450,000 ❶	320,000 ❶	
Revaluation Reserve	(W 7)		143,200 ❸	
Profit and Loss Balance			340,420	803,620
				803,620

Workings

1	**Customers' fees** – amount received	262,600	
	Add advance deposits	5,500	
	Add fees due	650	
	Less fees prepaid 31/12/2002	(4,000)	264,750
2	**Light and heat** – amount paid	2,900	
	Add stock – heating oil 1/1/2002	660	
	Add electricity due 31/12/2002	290	
	Less stock – heating oil 1/1/2002	(360)	
	Less charge to shop	(220)	3,270
3	**Purchases** (38,600 + 1,600 – 1,450)		38,750
4	**Loan Interest** – paid	6,800	
	Less interest due 1/1/2002 for 1 year @ €400 per month	4,800	2,000
5	**Depreciation** – Buildings & grounds 2% × (520,000 + 80,000)		12,000
	– Equipment 20% × (90,000 + 16,000)		21,200
	– Furniture 20% × (25,000)		5,000
6	**Contract Cleaning** – amount paid	2,700	
	Add amount prepaid 1/1/2002	300	
	Less amount 31/12/2002	(400)	2,600
7	**Revaluation Reserve**		
	Buildings (700,000–600,000 including extension)	100,000	
	Depreciation (31,200 + 12,000)	43,200	143,200

Question 7 – Incomplete Records

(a)

50

Balance Sheet as at 31 December 2002

		€	€
Intangible Assets			
Goodwill			40,000 ❸
Fixed Assets			
Buildings (290,000 + 250,000)		540,00 ❸	
Equipment		12,000 ❸	552,000
Financial Assets			
Investments			7,575 ❹
			599,575
Current Assets			
Stock at 31 December 2002	17,200 ❶		
Trade Debtors	34,300 ❶		
Bank	68,462 ❶		
Rates prepaid	2,700 ❹	122,662	
Less Creditors: amounts falling due within 1 year			
Creditors	29,900 ❶		
Interest due	1,500 ❸		
Electricity due	560 ❷	(31,960)	
Working Capital			90,702
			690,277
Financed by			
Creditors: amounts falling due after more than 1 year			
Loan			300,000 ❷
Capital – Balance at 1/1/2002		350,000 ❷	
Add Capital introduced		2,500 ❸	
Less Drawings **W 10**		(23,215) ❿	329,285
			629,285
Add Net Profit **W 1**			60,992
Capital Employed			690,277 ❼

(b) **40**

Trading and Profit and Loss Account for year ended 31 December 2002

		€	€
Sales	**W 3**		440,905 ❷
Less Cost of goods sold			
Stock at 1 January 2002		16,700 ❷	
Add Purchases (270,243–5,200)	**W 5**	265,043 ❷	
		281,743	
Less Stock 31 December 2002		(17,200) ❷	
Cost of sales	**W 4**		264,543 ❷
Gross Profit	**W 2**		176,362 ❷
Add Investment income			75 ❸
			176,437
Less Expenses			
Wages and general expenses	**W 6**	95,750 ❻	
Light and heat	**W 7**	5,820 ❻	
Rates	**W 8**	10,500 ❻	
Interest	**W 9**	3,375 ❻	115,445
Net Profit	**W 1**		60,992 ❶

(c) **10**

O'Higgins should keep a detailed cash book and general ledger supported by appropriate subsidiary day books. This would enable O'Higgins to prepare an accurate trading and profit and loss account and therefore would avoid reliance on estimates.

Workings

			€	€
1	**Net profit for year (balancing figure in balance sheet)**			
	Total net assets		690,277	
	Less Loan		(300,000)	
	Less capital after drawings and before profit		(329,285)	60,992
2	**Gross profit**			
	Net profit + expenses – gains	= (60,987 + 115,450 – 75)		176,362
3	**Sales**			
	Gross profit = 40% of sales	= 176,362 × 2.5		440,905
4	**Cost of sales**			
	Sales less gross profit	= 440,905 – 176,362		264,543
5	**Purchases**			
	Cost of sales + closing stock – opening stock	264,543 + 17,200 – 16,700		265,043

6	**Wages and general expenses** – amount paid	98,000	
	Add college fees 30% of €4,500	1,350	
	Less wages due at 1/1/2002	(3,600)	95,750
7	**Light and heat** – amount paid	7,200	
	Add electricity due 31/12/2002	560	
	Less drawings	(1,940)	
	Profit and loss account		5,820
8	**Rates – amount paid**	10,800	
	Add rates prepaid 1/1/2002	2,400	
	Less rates prepaid 31/12/2002	(2,700)	
	Profit and loss account		10,500
9	**Interest** – amount paid	3,000	
	Add interest due	1,500	
	Less drawings	(1,125)	
	Profit and loss account		3,375
10	**Drawings**		
	College fees – family member	3,150	
	Equipment	4,000	
	Drawings of stock	5,200	
	Cash	7,800	
	Light and heat	1,940	
	Interest	1,125	23,215

Question 8 – Costing

(a) **30**

Purchases in Units		**Cost Price €**	**Purchases at Cost €**
4,200	@	€7	29,400
3,200	@	€7	22,400
2,700	@	€8	21,600
2,300	@	€9	20,700
12,400			**94,100**

Sales in Units		**Selling Price €**	**Sales Value €**
2,400	@	€11	26,400
4,150	@	€12	49,800
3,900	@	€13	50,700
10,450			**126,900**

Closing Stock in units

Opening Stock	4,400
Add Purchases	12,400
	16,800
Less Sales	10,450
Closing Stock	**6,350**

Closing Stock in €

			€
2,300	@	€9	20,700
2,700	@	€8	21,600
1,350	@	€7	9,450
6,350			51,750 ⓯

Trading Account for year ending 31 December 2002

	€	€
Sales		126,900 ❸
Less cost of goods sold		
Opening stock	30,800 ❷	
Purchases	94,100 ❸	
	124,900	
Less Closing stock	51,750 ❸	73,150
Gross Profit		53,750 ❹

50

(b)

Calculation of Product Cost and Selling price

		€	€
Direct Materials			6,450.00 ❸
Direct wages:			
Department X	(90 hours @ €11)	990 ❸	
Department Y	(180 hours @ €12)	2,160 ❸	
Department Z	(50 hours @ €10)	500 ❸	3,650.00
Variable overheads			
Department X	(90 hours @ €18)	1,620.00 ❸	
Department Y	(180 hours @ €16)	2,880.00 ❸	
Department Z	(50 hours @ €20)	1,000.00 ❸	5,500.00
Fixed overheads			
Department X	(90 hours @ €8.50)	765 ❸	
Department Y	(180 hours @ €7.50)	1,350 ❸	
Department Z	(50 hours @ €4.00)	200 ❸	2,315.00
General Administration overhead (320 hours @ €4.50)			1,440.00 ❹
Total Cost =	75% of selling price		19,355.00 ❷
Profit =	25% of selling price		6,451.67
Selling Price =	100%		25,806.67 ❷

To establish the selling price for the purpose of tendering ❼

To control costs – budget versus actual ❺
To help planning and decision making
To ascertain the value of closing stock in order to prepare final accounts

Question 9

80

(i)

Direct materials	❶ Variable
Direct wages	❶ Variable
Production overheads	❷ Mixed
Other overhead costs	❷ Mixed
Administration expenses	❷ Mixed

(ii) Production overheads

	Units	**Total cost**
	€	**€**
High	17,000	110,000
Low	11,000	74,000
Difference	6,000	36,000

The variable cost of 6,000 units is €36,000, therefore the variable cost per unit is €6. ❻

	€	**€**	**€**
	55%	**70%**	**85%**
Total production overhead cost	74,000	92,000	110,000
Variable cost (Units × €6)	66,000	84,000	102,000
Therefore fixed cost	8,000	8,000	8,000 ❻

(iii) Other overhead costs

	Units	**Total Cost**
	€	**€**
High	17,000	54,000
Low	11,000	36,000
Difference	6,000	18,000

The variable cost of 6,000 units is €18,000, therefore the variable cost per unit is €3. ❻

	€	**€**	**€**
	55%	**70%**	**85%**
Total other overhead costs at	36,000	45,000	54,000
Variable cost (Units × €3)	33,000	42,000	51,000
Therefore, fixed cost	3,000	3,000	3,000 ❻

(iv) Production overheads at the required flexible budgeted level of 96% – (19,200 units)

	€
Variable cost (19,200 units × €6)	115,200
Fixed cost	8,000
Total cost	123,200 *

Other overhead costs at the required flexible budgeted level of 96% – (19,200 units).

	€
Variable cost (19,200 units × €3)	57,600
Fixed cost	3,000
Total cost	60,600 *

Construction of a flexible budget for a 96% activity level.

		Flexible Budget
Activity level		**96%**
Units		**19,200**
		€
Direct materials	(€13 × 19,200)	249,600 ❸
Direct wages	(€9 × 19,200)	172,800 ❸
Production overheads	(€6 × 19,200) + 8,000	*123,200 ❻
Administration overheads (fixed)		29,000 ❷
Other overhead costs	(€3 × 19,200) + 3,000	*60,600 ❻
Total cost (78% of sales)		635,200

(v) Flexible Budget In Marginal Costing Format

	€	€
Sales		814,359 ❶
Less Variable costs		
Direct materials	249,600 ❶	
Direct wages	172,800 ❶	
Variable production costs	115,200 ❶	
Other overhead costs	57,600 ❶	595,200
Contribution ❶		219,159
Less Fixed costs		
Production costs	8,000 ❶	
Selling and distribution costs	3,000 ❶	
Administration costs	29,000 ❶	40,000
Profit		179,159 ❸

(vi) Principal Budget Factor – Often referred to as the limiting budget factor or the key budget factor. ❼

This is the factor that limits output and therefore prevents continuous expansion. Usually the principal budget factor is sales demand. The principal budget factor could be some other limiting factor such as availability of materials.

Why prepare a flexible budget and what does it show?

To compare budgeted costs and actual costs at the same level of activity ❻
To compare like with like
To help in controlling costs or to plan product levels

They show whether actual costs exceeded or were less than budgeted costs. (variances) ❸